"A very readable and inspiring book for busy Christians who need to overcome a compartmentalized life."

—*Dr. Michael J. Naughton, Moss Chair in Catholic Social Thought, University of St. Thomas*

"*Hope for the Workplace* captures the Christian truths by which I sought to live my life as a husband, father, football coach, and owner of a NASCAR race team. I would recommend this book to anyone who asks the question, 'Is it possible to live my faith in the business world?' Bill Dalgetty offers hope for any Christian who has ever struggled with living out his or her faith in the workplace."

—*Joe Gibbs, former Washington Redskins head coach and NASCAR championship team owner*

"How does God value our work? Bill Dalgetty provides a comprehensive understanding in *Hope for the Workplace*. Bill combines years of personal experience, personal study, and application to this work. I highly recommend *Hope for the Workplace*."

—*Os Hillman, president, Marketplace Leaders Ministries, and author of* The 9 to 5 Window; *and* Faith & Work

"*Hope for the Workplace* offers some great insights and firsthand accounts of conduct and decisions that fit very well in setting the ethics guidelines in companies of all sizes. I would have found it a valuable resource in guiding the companies I have been privileged to lead over the past thirty years."

—*C. J. Waylan, PhD, retired president, GTE Spacenet Corp, Vienna, Virginia*

"What a book! I love the style—crisp, filled with inspiring stories, replete with quotes from Scripture and leading figures in Christianity!"

—*The Reverend Mark Moretti, St. John's Catholic Church, Warrenton, Virginia*

HOPE

for the

WORKPLACE

CHRIST IN YOU

BILL DALGETTY

Scriptures taken from the Holy Bible, New International Version®, NIV®. Copyright © 1973, 1978, 1984, 2011 by Biblica, Inc.™ Used by permission of Zondervan. All rights reserved worldwide. www.zondervan.com The "NIV" and "New International Version" are trademarks registered in the United States Patent and Trademark Office by Biblica, Inc.™

Published by Zacchaeus Publications, Vienna, Virginia.

Cover image: shutterstock.com
Cover design and interior layout: Creative Editorial Solutions

ISBN: 978-1-939909-06-0 (soft cover)
ISBN: 978-1-939909-07-7 (e-book)

Printed in the United States of America

8 7 6 5 1 2 3 4

DEDICATION

To my wife, Marilynn, whose words and example led me to meet Jesus Christ in a new and personal way one October evening many years ago. It was a watershed moment that opened the door to a life in the Spirit in our marriage, family and my professional life.

To my children, Elizabeth, Jenny, Susan and Stephen and their families whose love and support have encouraged me to persist in writing this book; and to our special needs daughter, Emily, whose smiles, hugs and love have drawn me closer to the Father.

To the men and women of Christians in Commerce who have accepted God's invitation to dwell in them and be the hope for their workplaces. Many of their stories illustrate the premise of this book that if we accept God's invitation to dwell in us, we can be the hope for business and commerce and transform our workplaces in how we relate to others, conduct ourselves with integrity and seek excellence in all that we do.

All royalties from this book will be donated to the ministry of Christians in Commerce International.

TABLE OF CONTENTS

ACKNOWLEDGMENTS

The germ of this book arose out of a seminar by the same name which was developed for Christians in Commerce International. Fellow Board member Steve Becker played a key role in developing some of the material for that seminar which has found its way into this book. Steve also provided valuable comments on the initial outline of the book and subsequent manuscript.

I want to thank Claudia Volkman for transforming a manuscript into a book with her professional editing, layout, and design efforts.

Many people reviewed the manuscript and offered helpful comments and suggestions: Patty Mitchell, Louis Grams, John Mooney, Bud Rose, Jerry Waylan, Bill Colegrove, The Reverend Mark Moretti, Dave Hazelton, Walt Seale, Tim and Celesta Rowland, Louise Paré of Servant Books, and Justin Bratnober. Special mention is given to the late John Jones, editorial director of the Crossroads Publishing Company, who offered valuable suggestions.

Finally, many thanks to my wife, Marilynn, who proofread early and final drafts, and whose love, encouragement and support sustained me throughout this endeavor.

FOREWORD

In 1977, the religious not-for-profit organization I was working for asked me to take responsibility for a group of for-profit businesses we owned. I quickly discovered that these businesses were all in deep financial trouble. I assembled a group of competent business owners and asked if they would serve on a board of directors of a holding company that would rebuild these businesses on sound business principles while reflecting the essential Christian values of the non-profit that owned them.

There was a long, nervous pause, and then one of the men at the table broke down and began to weep. He explained that his own business was deep in debt and ready to collapse. One by one, the others told similar stories of crisis, failure, and profound frustration.

I was deeply moved by the desperation affecting these experienced businesspeople. I was stunned as they told me how difficult it was to try to be faithful to the Gospel in their respective workplaces. For the most part, they said that they didn't know how to do that, and more than a few commented that their churches were happy to befriend them when their businesses were doing well, but when things got tough and help was sought, the responses amounted to blank stares or worse.

I could not get the plight of this group out of my mind. As I prayed for them, I found myself being lead to Scripture passages that seemed very relevant to the needs of this group. I asked them if they would like to get together to talk about the issues they had raised, and they agreed.

Soon we were meeting on a weekly basis for breakfast, a talk on some compelling passage of Scripture, and a discussion of how that passage might impact the way each person approached their work. Soon, others began coming to our meetings.

About the same time friends in South Bend, Indiana, and Phoenix, Arizona, were having a similar experience with business people in their communities. Together we began to work toward the vision of an organization that would take people through an intensive introductory retreat and then build long-term, supportive relationships. Calling it Christians in Commerce, our purpose was to bring Christ into the marketplace.

Bill Dalgetty's enthusiasm for the vision and work was one of the most encouraging things to happen to us in those early years. With his deep and lively faith, he embodied much of what we were trying to teach and promote through CIC. Right up to the present, Bill has been a major influence in the development of Christians in Commerce before, during, and after his tenure as president of the organization.

Bill's own life experience prepared him wonderfully to bring Christ into the marketplace and to help others do so as well. His warm and compassionate personality equipped him to seek out and take in the stories of countless other men and women as they took up the same mission. All of that is reflected here in this book. They are stories of Christ taking on human flesh and blood in our own time to minister love, kindness, understanding, mercy, and forgiveness again and again.

We live in a world that constantly tries to isolate our faith in Jesus Christ as a private, "interior" experience. Nothing could be further from the vision and mission that Jesus gave his people, and gave to men and women in commerce in particular. In a pluralistic culture, there are often necessary (and some not so necessary) restraints on what we can say in public, in the marketplace, but there should be no restraint on living lives of justice, honesty, mercy, forgiveness, or love—in other words, living as Christ.

There should be no restraint on treating those over us, our peers, or those who work under us with the profound respect due to each of God's children and with the full measure of love that originates in God, who is love. It has been said that the Gospel should be proclaimed in season and out—and that sometimes we might use words to do that. In other words, it's not about what we say, but what we do and who we are.

We can sometimes tend to get our words out ahead of our actions. *Hope for the Workplace* is not about words, but about actions. The challenge to bring Christ into the marketplace has never been greater. It's a challenge that can only be met by women and men who freely give themselves to Jesus Christ and to his people, day in and day out.

As Bill demonstrates again and again in this book, it can be done and is being done.

—Louis Grams, *co-founder of Christians in Commerce*

Introduction

HOPE IN SPITE OF THE HEADLINES

In spite of over a decade of headlines that give the impression business is rife with greed and corruption, more and more Christians are making a difference in their workplaces. You won't read about them in the newspapers or see them on the nightly news, but they are bringing about change through their everyday actions. They are making a difference in how they relate to the people around them, in conduct marked by integrity, and in the excellence they strive for in their work. They are transforming their workplaces and building God's kingdom "on earth as it is in heaven" (Mt. 6:10). Here are two examples of the nearly fifty real life stories that make up the larger story of this book.

Transforming a Company in Trouble

John Aden became CEO of Mac Tools in 2000 at age thirty-three. Mac Tools was a broken business at the time and required significant restructuring. After joining the company, John and his team were faced with having to significantly reduce the size of the workforce. In the first quarter of 2003, the company had to lay off over a thousand employees—54 percent of the total workforce. There were significant challenges as they worked through the details of the restructuring plan, which included dealing with some difficult relationships on the company's management team.

John grew up in a Christian family and attended Christian schools in grade school and junior high. However, in 2003 he met the Lord in a new way. While studying Henry Blackaby's *Experiencing God*, John learned there was a difference between "religion" and having a close relationship with God. Afterwards he realized that there was a huge gap in his life between Sunday and Monday. As John drew closer to God, his values began to change. God changed him from the inside out, and ultimately John started bringing those values to his work.

In his first year as CEO, John made his entrance at a large gathering of employees on a Harley Davidson motorcycle, riding down the center aisle and up onto the stage. In the year following his new walk with the Lord, at a similar meeting he acknowledged to his employees that he had too much pride and too little humility, that his leadership lacked stewardship and transparency, and he asked their support in making changes.

Next, John took his management team off-site for several days to examine the current company values. They came up with six new values, all biblically based. And then they did an interesting thing: They decided not to publish or talk about the new values of accountability, respect, honor, teamwork, integrity, and continuous improvement. Instead, they decided to live the values in their day-to-day interactions and allow the rest of the company to discover them through their example.

According to John, the results were amazing; they brought about an entire transformation of the company in terms of how management related to employees and how employees related to customers. John says the Lord showed him, "You don't even have to say my name and I can work." Because John allowed God to dwell in him and change him, God could work through him in cooperation with the Spirit to bring transformation to his company.

The Face of Christ in an Urban School

Jan teaches in an urban middle school of almost a thousand seventh and eighth graders. Her students originate from over seventy different countries, representing languages, cultures and religions from around the globe. Some of her students come from homeless shelters. Many return home to empty apartments where their parents work twelve to sixteen hours a day. By the age of thirteen, some have full responsibility for younger siblings or go home to parent a dysfunctional parent. Some bilingual students serve as their family translator, and others work all weekend to help support a family business.

Jan observes, "Not only are students often unable to complete their schoolwork, I see them struggling with depression, isolation, fear, anxiety, chaos, addictions, and hopelessness. As a public school teacher, I cannot openly evangelize or tell them about God's love; I would be fired or sued.

"What I can offer them is the face of Christ. In my classroom they have come to expect fairness, kindness, and consistency. They know I have expectations for appropriate speech toward one another, and I hold them accountable to it. They know that we play by the rules and my expectations are high, but they will be safe.

They have a place where trust has been established, and their accomplishments, no matter how small, are met with praise and encouragement. Although they may not know it, Christ is truly at work as they respond to his love. Students have told me that my classroom is unusual because they are treated with respect."

One year, due to staffing changes, Jan was given a unique opportunity to hand-select a small class of thirteen boys. She chose low-achieving, struggling readers that the system had simply shuffled along for years. Jan says, "I began in small ways by building a classroom community, providing a positive educational experience, and earning their trust. I show them the face of Christ simply through our routine daily interactions.

"In just a few months, these rough-and-tumble street kids have gelled into a cohesive class that is moving forward. They are positive and motivated, and they genuinely look out for one another, both academically and socially. They have made it clear that they want to stay in this group for the rest of the year, and with pride, they call themselves 'The Brotherhood.' Time will tell if their academics will match their attitudinal gains, but much of the groundwork is already in place. What I do know is that our Father loves each of them as his own."

Jan does not mention the name of Jesus in her classroom. She does not pray out loud. She does not share her Catholic faith. Yet she is bringing the presence of God to her students by the way she treats them with respect and dignity, speaks the truth, sets the rules and expectations, intercedes for them in prayer, and loves them. Jan is allowing God to become incarnate in her though the power of the Holy Spirit in order to bring Christ's love and care to her students.

Though this is a different kind of workplace than we see in John's story, God is working through Jan to transform her students and bring order out of chaos. Just as John brought transformation to his company, Jan is bringing transformation and hope to her classroom. How this is happening and its impact on all kinds of workplaces is the subject of this book.

God's Solution

Living out one's Christian faith in today's workplace is met with many challenges: Competitive pressures to do more with less, difficult relationships, the blurring of right and wrong, the focus on self to the detriment of others, and the difficulty of balancing the demands of work and family are just a few examples. Adding to these challenges is the tendency to separate one's faith from one's work.

God has a solution to these challenges. It involves accepting his offer to dwell in us and have a personal relationship with him through his son, Jesus Christ. As St. Paul says, "The mystery that has been kept hidden for ages and generations…is Christ in you, the hope of glory" (Col 1:26, 27). Christ in us is our hope—and the hope for the workplace. Through our "yes" to God's offer of friendship and the release of the power of the Holy Spirit in our lives, God enables us to bring his presence to bear on the circumstances of our work life.

Our work is important to God. It has always been a part of his plan for creation. It has always been his intention that we would partner with him in tending the garden of creation, bringing forth civilization and moving it forward to the day when he "may be all in all" (1 Cor 15:28). God never intended for us to separate our relationship with him from our work. He desires to be present in our workplaces through us just as much as he desires to be present in our families and churches through us. The stories in this book illustrate how integrity, excellence, leadership, relationships, sacrifice, work environment, forgiveness, and healing play out in real life.

HOPE FOR THE WORKPLACE

There is a common notion among many Christians that the kingdom of God is only something we can experience after we lead a good life, die, and go to heaven. But so much of what Jesus said to the people of his day, particularly in his parables, exhorted them to do something with this life in order to advance the creation God had inaugurated and Jesus had redeemed. Forty-five of Jesus' fifty-two parables have a workplace context.[1]

All Christians have the opportunity to bring transformation and hope to their workplaces by having an ongoing relationship with God, experiencing the power of the Holy Spirit, seeking God's will in their daily conduct, and allowing God to work through them to bring love, truth, justice, and excellence to the people and circumstances of their lives. The pages that follow will reveal how you can experience this transformation and hope in your workplace.

Blessed John Paul II said, "The lay faithful are called by God so that they, led by the spirit of the Gospel, might contribute to the sanctification of the world, as from within like leaven, by fulfilling their own particular duties. Thus, especially in this way of life, resplendent in faith, hope and charity they manifest Christ to others."[2]

I believe the call to be Christ and to bring his presence to the workplace is a universal call applicable to all Christians. As a practicing Catholic, I have relied on Scripture and both Catholic and Protestant resources in this book. This message is for all Christians, so the experiences of both Catholics and Protestants are included here, which illustrate how much commonality there is in our varied perspectives and traditions.

Similarly, this book is for Christians at all levels of the workplace spectrum, including employees, managers, executives, and business owners. It has application as much to the grass roots employee as to the middle manager or senior executive.

Finally, questions for personal reflection or small group discussion appear at the end of each chapter.

Chapter One

GROANS HEARD IN
THE WORKPLACE

Today's workplace is intense and demanding. Increased global competition and numerous advances in technology have created pressure to be more productive and competitive. Consolidation, restructuring, and layoffs have resulted in fewer employees being asked to do more than ever before.

Jill Andresky Fraser, in her book, *White Collar Sweatshop*, talks about how year after year of cost cutting, lagging raises, declining benefits, and increased workloads have taken a toll on white collar workers throughout corporate America.[1] She offers the following examples:

THE 5:29 P.M. COMMUTER TRAIN to Scarsdale is jammed; usually it's standing room only for the half hour it takes to reach the upscale suburb from New York City's Grand Central Station. During the ride, Gemma, a marketing executive, phones her office for messages, not once but twice, returning as many calls as possible in quick succession from her cell phone. She keeps her voice low, tries to conclude the calls quickly; there are too many of them, after all, and her seatmates are apt to send irritated looks her way. But she makes them anyway, despite longing to doze off. "It's the only way I can leave my office most days at five o'clock and get home to have dinner with my family," Gemma says. By seven-thirty, once dinner is done, it's back to those phone calls. While her children wrap up the last pages of their homework, Gemma again checks her voicemail, taking time to respond to as many calls as necessary. As the evening winds to a close, clients may call too. "When a client needs you, they need you," she sighs. "I honestly feel that I never relax."

LEONARD, WITH A CAREER that has spanned important positions with three separate high-tech companies, experiences the pressure of his twelve-hour workdays and managerial responsibilities, which have included supervising numerous layoffs during the past decade. Although his six-figure salary and benefits are more than he ever could have wanted, it has left him feeling more like a survivor than a star. "The philosophy now is that you have to squeeze more and more out of people," says Leonard. "I have to do more and more with less. I had a call one day telling me I had to lay off ten people. There was no discussion. It wasn't appropriate for me to say no or yes. We laid those people off, so now I'm in litigation with some of them. They're mad. I understand that. But here is the reality: If I don't do it, I'm gone. That's clear. I feel I am too old to start again, but too young to hang it up. The only way I can protect myself is by trying to out-perform everybody else. That means working harder and harder."

As these examples indicate, it is not uncommon to see insecurity, resentment, and unhappiness among employees. Rivalries thrive. Employers and employees are often at odds with each other. Products and services can fall short of their promises. Greed can drive daily decisions.

Groans Heard in the Workplace

We see the impact in the headlines of corporate deceit and wrongdoing. We see it in the faces of people at work—faces often weary, puzzled, living without any clear understanding of what life is about. We witness the strain on families, faith, and society. Many Christians compartmentalize their lives and check their faith at the door. Christian morals that would govern other areas of life are ignored or set aside in the workplace. This is often manifested in subtle ways, such as acquiescing to a questionable accounting practice or inflating the miles driven on an expense account.

Cynthia Cooper, the vice president of Internal Audit for WorldCom who discovered massive fraudulent accounting in 2002, says in her book, *Extraordinary Circumstances*, "Most of the people who participated in the WorldCom fraud were ordinary, middle-class Americans. They had no prior criminal records and never imagined they would be confronted with such life-altering choices. They were mothers and fathers who went to work to support their families, spent their weekends going to their children's activities and to church, and were respected within their communities." In speculating on the motivation of those who participated in the fraud, she observed: "Top-level executives, used to seeing their company win, felt a sense of pride, and didn't want World-Com to fail on their watch. Greed may have been a factor for the executives who had their personal fortunes on the line." Mid-level employees "felt pressured and afraid that they would lose their jobs if they didn't go along."[2]

We see this same kind of compartmentalizing when faith does not seem to impact a Christian who takes credit for a subordinate's work, records false numbers on a maintenance log, participates in gossip that damages a colleague's character, or is fearful of telling the boss what he or she doesn't want to hear.

These tendencies feed off the problems we see in our culture at large—a dominant concern for self, moral confusion, empty measures of success, and a world that acts as if God does not exist. We will examine each of these problems so that we can come to recognize them in ourselves and the world around us. This will help us better understand how God wants us to respond to the circumstances of our lives and to him.

Concern for Self

Human nature tends to be inherently selfish. G. K. Chesterton observed that original sin is the one Christian doctrine that is empirically validated by centuries of human history.[3] This condition, if left unchecked by God's presence, leads to greed, lust, exploitation, isolation, and many other negative consequences.

A dominant focus on self has many adverse impacts on the workplace. We see ambition at the expense of others, envy, manipulation, unwillingness to serve or sacrifice, lack of cooperation, and compromise of values, to name only a few. The importance of others is diminished. Fellow employees, family, community, country, social order, and one's employer become a means to personal ends. The good of the team, the good of the company, and the good of the family are subverted to an attitude of "me first."

Early in my career as a young attorney for Mobil Corporation, I thought I was on an upward track, and my ambition to succeed began to dominate the choices in my life. Everything else—my wife, my children, and my relationship with God—began to take second place. I continued to go to Mass every Sunday and I loved my family, but my career and moving up the corporate ladder became paramount in my life.

Through God's grace and mercy, along with the example of my wife, Marilynn, that all changed one evening when I turned over the mixed priorities and sin in my life to Jesus Christ. We were living in New York at the time. A friend had invited my wife to a Week of Renewal being conducted in a nearby Catholic parish. It started on a Sunday evening, running five nights through Thursday evening. My wife had asked me to join her, but I declined saying that I had a briefcase full of work. Each night when she came home, I noticed how happy she seemed. She would invite me again to the next night's program, but I continued to decline. On Wednesday evening when she walked in the door, she was absolutely radiant and said something that astounded me: "I believe I could forgive almost anything of anyone." I thought to myself, "I've got to see what is going on here," and I decided to join her the next evening.

The final evening included a talk and a healing Mass. At one point the priest who was leading the service asked everyone to kneel down, close their eyes, and imagine that they were somewhere all alone with no one present except Jesus. Then he asked us to give to Jesus whatever need we might have—physical healing, sin in our life, the healing of a relationship, etc. "Give it to Jesus," he said, "and ask him to take it from you."

Well, I dutifully knelt down, closed my eyes and, for whatever reason, imagined that I was on a lonely country road south of Kansas City, Missouri, on the way to my wife's grandmother's farm. Jesus was standing there with me. I looked at him and said, "Lord, you know what is going on in my life—the disorder and sin.... Would you take it from me?"

As soon as I asked the question, I heard him say, "Yes." I immediately felt a sense of release rush through my body. The proverbial weight was being lifted from my shoulders. I couldn't believe it was happening. It was as if I were transported by the Spirit to that country road to meet Jesus face-to-face. It was so real that I can still describe every detail, even the architecture of the farmhouse adjacent to where we were standing.

Back at the church, the priest then said a beautiful prayer and went on with the Mass and the rest of the evening's program. At first I was elated and felt such a sense of release. But as the evening progressed, I started to think about what I had experienced. I began to wonder if it really happened. Was it just a figment of my imagination? I started to debate with myself. One part of me said I was just letting my imagination get carried away, and another part said that what had just happened was as real as anything I had ever experienced.

After the program concluded, prayer teams were stationed around the church to pray with people for various needs. I thought about asking for additional prayer—a little insurance that what happened really happened, but I was reluctant. Finally I got the courage to walk up to a three-person team made up of a priest, a nun, and another woman. They asked me what they could pray for, and I said, "Well, my mother has arthritic knees that are really crippling her, and…I would like prayers for a spiritual healing (a phrase I had heard that evening for the first time, and my way of being as vague as possible about my need and struggle)."

The priest said, "Sister, you pray for Mom's knees, and I'll pray for the spiritual healing." They laid hands on me, anointed my forehead with oil, and said a beautiful prayer. I thanked them and, as I started to walk away, the priest took hold of my arm and said, "You don't believe." I looked at him, startled, and he said, "Oh, you believe in God, but you don't believe he has healed you. God does not think you are half as bad as you think you are. If you will just accept his forgiveness and love, great things will start happening in your life."

Well, if I was moved by the earlier experience of meeting Jesus on the country road, I was absolutely overwhelmed by these words, for here was a man I had never met before speaking to the innermost secrets and concerns of my heart. How could he know? Who told him to say these things? In fact, I said, "Would you say that again?" The nun said to me, "You may not understand all that God is doing right now, but he will give you understanding."

The next morning I awoke with an incredible sense of peace, and God began the long process of changing my life. The first thing he did was give me the desire to be reconciled with anyone I might have offended. He also gave me an intense desire to read Scripture. Over the next few months, I read the Bible from cover to cover as I commuted on the train each day in and out of New York City. I acquired a new love for my Church. Prayers that I had heard at Mass for years took on new life. God blessed my marriage and family in unexpected ways. And finally, I began to seek God's presence in every aspect of my life, including my professional life.

Christians are not immune from letting concerns of self override the concerns of others or the needs of the larger organization or family of which they are a part. Personal agendas, selfishness, territorialism, competiveness, and conflict can be found among Christians and Christian organizations just as in society at large.

Only with the presence of Jesus in our lives are we able to overcome our inclination to put self first. Without Jesus, even our best of intentions will likely fail. Jesus said, "I am the vine; you are the branches. If a man remains in me and I in him, he will bear much fruit; apart from me you can do nothing" (Jn 15:5). Apart from Jesus, we can do nothing. We may think we can, but we cannot live the life to which God calls us without Jesus.

My ambition to be a successful corporate attorney pushed aside the relationship that I had previously had with God through my Catholic faith and dulled my sensitivities to the people most important in my life—my wife and children. By ambition, I am not talking about seeking excellence, which is part of being a good steward of the time, talents, and resources God gives us. Instead, I am referring to ambition in the sense of an inordinate desire or lust for position, prestige, and power. Like much sin, ambition starts in small ways and then feeds upon itself and grows with ever-increasing self-focus until we become blind to its impact on ourselves and those around us. I will be forever grateful for God's mercy and grace, which led me to encounter Jesus on that country road.

Moral Confusion

The many revelations of fraudulent accounting practices by a multitude of companies in recent years testify to a moral crisis in corporate America. Entire companies have been destroyed (Enron, WorldCom, Arthur Anderson, Tyco, Global Crossing, for example), employees' lives have been shattered (with jobs lost and 401Ks wiped out), and shareholders have lost billions of dollars. For many business leaders, the clear line between right and wrong has become blurred. Moral values have become relative, based upon personal choice and societal whims instead of God's revealed truths.

Taking a Stand for Accounting Integrity

Douglas went to work for a new company in San Jose, California, that resulted from a merger of four other companies. After the new company went public, both management and investors carefully watched the company's first quarter results. As the end of the quarter drew near, it appeared that earnings were going to fall short of projections. Management decided that it would pre-bill some of the next quarter sales so that earnings for the current quarter would meet projections.

When Douglas learned of this, he protested to his boss that he could not be a part of any accounting manipulations that might result in the misstatement of first-quarter earnings. His boss replied that there was nothing he could do since the decision had been made by senior management. Douglas knew the president of the company, so he told his boss that he was going to call the president to express his concerns.

When the president responded that the company lawyers and accountants had approved the proposed action, Douglas reminded the president that integrity was at the forefront of the company's new vision statement and that this action did not live up to that vision.

Because of Douglas' courage and willingness to stand up for accounting integrity, the president reversed the decision the next day, and the earnings were reported correctly.

In a 2005 global study conducted by the Human Resource Institute for the American Management Association, 1,121 executives and managers were asked what was most important in ensuring an ethical culture. Leaders' support and modeling of ethical behavior was the most favored answer, with 93.5 percent responding that it was "extremely or highly important."[4]

Michael Novak, in his book, *The Spirit of Democratic Capitalism,* says that of all the systems devised by men, capitalism is the one most likely to lift the poor out of poverty, but he adds, "It cannot thrive apart from the moral culture that nourishes the virtues and values on which it depends."[5]

Honesty over Job Security

Pat Gangi had just completed her master's degree in Instructional Design and was experiencing difficulty finding work in her field. Finally she was hired to complete the last six months of work on a three-year federal grant at a small college in the southeast. The purpose of the grant was to build a media center in the college's Agriculture Department, develop effective policies and procedures, and motivate department professors to create more engaging learning methods using media center facilities and services. Part of Pat's work was to conduct surveys on the impact and effectiveness of the grant and then write an evaluation which would be sent to the federal agency supplying the grant.

When Pat presented the report to the university, the department chair responsible for overseeing the grant asked Pat to remove certain negative findings coming out of the surveys relating to the faculty's lack of use of the media center in their teaching methods. The department chair did not want the college—or himself—to look bad, which led to his request to revise the report.

Pat says, "How could I not report all of the findings? When I balked at signing a revised report, the department chair became manipulative and coercive. He knew that I had been looking for work for a long time, and he reminded me that they were seriously considering offering me a permanent position after the grant ended. He implied that if I went along with his request, I could continue to work for the university. He also clearly implied that my lack of cooperation would make that post-grant job disappear."

"If you insist that I sign a revised report," she told the chairman, "you will have my resignation in the morning." As she later reflected, "This was my first professional work after receiving my degree. If I started my career this way, how could it not have an impact on how I conducted myself later on?"

The department chair relented and forwarded the report to the federal government as Pat had written it. But as he had indicated, the subsequent job with the university never materialized.

While Pat demonstrated integrity in refusing to change the findings of the report, it was costly to her. "It took me four months to find another job," she said. "However, sharing this challenging experience in a subsequent job interview helped me get a new and even better job."

Most of us would acknowledge that our moral base is being undermined, but in reality a strong moral base is dependent upon each of us. The tragedy is when individual Christians don't react when they see unethical behavior taking place around them. They limit the presence and power of God working through them, and they do not realize that God is calling them to join with him in building his kingdom in their workplaces.

God doesn't just call business leaders, but all workers. Middle management is the moral backbone of every business. Middle managers have more frontline influence than most upper management. They can affect not only those who work for them, but also those for whom they work, as in the stories of Douglas and Pat. If all Christians allowed the presence of God to be manifested in their lives and work, they could dramatically change a declining moral base.

Empty Measures of Success

Greg Aitkens joined a major West Coast life insurance company and was trained in its home office in Newport Beach, California. In his first year he qualified for their prestigious "Million Dollar Roundtable," a distinction that only the top 2 percent of life insurance agents achieve. His agency named him "Rookie Agent of the Year."

Each year he qualified for the annual sales leaders' conventions—lavish events that were held in London, Hong Kong, Monte Carlo, and Hawaii. One year, while at the annual convention in Monte Carlo (a black-tie affair in a beautiful room overlooking Monte Carlo), Greg vowed to himself that "someday" he too would sell enough to be one of those agents who would be paraded up the aisle to the stage for "recognition."

Each year, however, the production standards to qualify were raised. Some years, Greg struggled with this and even found himself "pushing" customers to buy enough so that he could qualify. He compromised the truth, telling lies at times just to ensure his "spot" at the convention.

One day he woke up and asked himself, "What am I doing? Why am I doing it? What am I building?" The success he was being offered was an illusion. He had bought into it, and now its emptiness was beginning to dawn on him. Worldly success was a moving target, one that kept eluding him just when it seemed within his grasp. In addition, none of the recognition had anything to do with the quality of service to his clients, careful planning, or the value to the purchaser. The only measurement was production—the number of policies sold, premiums gathered, commissions paid, and increase in revenues.

Compromising his integrity was taking a toll on Greg. The artificial smile, not being totally forthcoming—it was all having an effect on him. It also affected his relationships with his wife, children, and close friends. He was irritable and moody much of the time. Even though Greg had become "successful" in the eyes of the world, he was unfulfilled and personally unhappy.

"Greed Began to Consume Me"

Todd Sinelli, in his book, *True Riches*, says: "After college, I defined success by how much money I could make. This was my target. I really thought that the more money I made, the more successful I would become. I wrote an eight-year plan when I was twenty-two. One of the things I wanted to do before age thirty was to become a millionaire. To be rich was my dream."

After completing graduate school, Todd wanted to get a job as a stock trader, but because of his lack of experience, no one would hire him. So he raised $20,000 by taking a $5,000 line of credit on four credit cards that he received after graduating. After diligent research, he invested in a few companies whose stock skyrocketed. Within six months, the $20,000 had turned into more than $100,000.

"It was amazing," said Todd. "Here I was, a twenty-four-year-old, making six figures in less than six months. As a reward to myself, I went out and traded my Jeep Wrangler for a Mercedes Benz. I paid the difference in cash.

"Greed began to consume me. Money became my sole desire.

The freedom to buy anything I wanted was intoxicating. When I first started trading, I thought if I made one hundred thousand dollars a year, that would be great. But you know what? After I made one hundred thousand dollars, I wanted five hundred thousand. After I had made five hundred thousand, I wanted a million. When I made a million, I wanted two. When I had two, I wanted five. I made my first million at the age of twenty-five. Within another year I was a multimillionaire. Looking back, it is clear that my hunger for riches was unfulfilling. I believed a lie."[6]

As the author of Ecclesiastes observes, "Whoever loves money never has money enough; whoever has wealth is never satisfied with his income" (Eccl 5:10). The initial views of success held by Greg and Todd are shared by many. More money means success because it supposedly gives us freedom and control. The world judges us by our possessions. How big is our house? How expensive is our car? Most corporate cultures view success in terms of span of responsibility. How many employees work for you? How big are your expense and capital budgets?

As both Greg and Todd came to realize, success defined only in terms of money, possessions, power, and pleasures is transitory. "None of these is ultimately fulfilling because none can answer that ultimate question of purpose," says Chuck Colson in his book, *How Now Shall We Live?* Colson concludes, "Knowing that we are fulfilling God's purpose is the only thing that really gives rest to the restless human heart."[7] Jesus said, "My food is to do the will of him who sent me" (Jn 4:34). Similarly, our success should be measured by how well we are fulfilling God's will for our lives, not by what position we hold or how much wealth we have accumulated.

In the Parable of the Rich Fool, Jesus said, "The ground

of a certain rich man produced a good crop. He thought to himself, 'What shall I do? I have no place to store my crops.' Then he said, 'This is what I'll do. I will tear down my barns and build bigger ones, and there I will store all my grain and goods.' And I'll say to myself, 'You have plenty of good things laid up for many years. Take life easy; eat, drink and be merry.' But God said to him, 'You fool! This very night your life will be demanded from you. Then who will get what you have prepared for yourself?' This is how it will be with anyone who stores up things for himself but is not rich toward God" (Lk 12:16-21).

We become rich toward God when we seek him, his friendship, and his will in all things. Money and position are not evil in themselves. It is our attitude and motivation toward money and wealth that causes us problems—or, as St. Paul says, it is "the love of money" that is the root of all kinds of evil. More specifically, he says, "People who want to get rich fall into temptation and a trap and into many foolish and harmful desires that plunge men into ruin and destruction" (1 Tim 6:9-10). Jesus says, "Seek first his kingdom and his righteousness, and all these things will be given to you as well" (Mt 6:33).

A World that Has Forgotten God

The world's approach to the foregoing problems speaks to us primarily from a secular perspective, often ignoring their underlying causes. Ever since the Age of Enlightenment began in the sixteenth century, humankind has been struggling with the idea that the human race, with its rational intelligence, ingenuity, energy, and will, can eventually solve most of the problems it faces. This view, of course, denies any role for the creator. And this leads to a serious problem: Many people act as if God does not exist.

Even those who acknowledge the existence of God often separate their faith from other aspects of their lives, particularly the workplace. The Second Vatican Council said, "This split between the faith which many profess and their daily lives deserves to be counted among the more serious errors of our age."[8] In commenting on this condition, Blessed John Paul II said, "A faith that does not affect a person's culture is a faith not fully embraced, not entirely thought out, not faithfully lived."[9]

A Changed Man, A Changed Company

Joe Blanco operates a dry-cleaning business in Chandler, Arizona. For several years he did this without much thought or concern for his customers or his employees. God was not a part of his life and certainly not a part of his business. As Joe observed, "I used to lie to my employees, and they would steal from me." His home life wasn't any better. Joe said, "I wasn't really there for my wife and kids. I drank too much and often would not go home until late at night."

One day one of Joe's customers invited him to a breakfast meeting of Christians in Commerce, an international ecumenical Christian ministry to the marketplace.[10] "At first I felt strange," Joe said, "but I was moved by what I saw in the men who attended. They were so genuine and supportive of each other, and so free to praise God. I had never seen anything like that before. Through these men I realized that God was calling me to change. At a subsequent weekend retreat, Joe said, "I experienced true forgiveness and acceptance, along with a great release of guilt.

"The Lord has blessed me so much since then," Joe continued. "He gave me a desire to love and serve my customers and to train and spend time with my employees. My customers say, 'You've changed!'

My employees now wear uniforms. They are polite to the customers. Last year, through a survey by the Southwest Dry Cleaners Association, my business was rated number one in customer service.

"One of the greatest blessings is my new relationship with my wife and kids. I am home every night now. My wife and I play games with our kids and spend a lot of time with each other. There is a new love in our family," Joe says.

Previously, Joe lived his life as if God did not exist or had no relevance to his life. This is not an uncommon situation in our society, even with people who have been baptized and raised as Christians. Today, Joe's life is very different. God is very much a part of every aspect of his life, including his business life and home life, and both are the better for it.

A Struggle against the Forces of Evil

Many in the workplace today are in denial about sin in their lives and their need for God. We are often passionate about our careers, money, and success but indifferent to the meaning of life and its purpose. Instead, we tend to fill our lives with possessions and other diversions, usually to meet some short-term desire. As St. Paul says, we "have exchanged the truth of God for a lie, and worshiped created things rather than the creator" (Rom 1:25).

What are we really seeing here? It is a struggle with evil and sin. It is a problem of humanity separating itself from its creator. All the issues discussed here reflect the powers of the world and the forces of evil. As we give in to self-centeredness, moral confusion, and success measured by power, possessions, and pleasures, we are actually feeding the powers of the world, and this has a cumulative effect on the workplace in which we find ourselves.

By 1999, WorldCom had become one of the largest telecom companies in the world with annual revenues of over $38 billion, employing some 100,000 people and operating in over sixty-five countries. On June 25, 2002, WorldCom announced that it had misstated its financial statements over the last five quarters by $3.8 billion, a sum that would eventually grow to $11 billion.[11]

Earnings had begun to decline and management was looking to reduce expenses. When they realized that they were paying too much for leased line costs that they weren't selling to customers, they decided to capitalize the line costs. This meant moving the line costs from their profit-and-loss statement (decreasing expenses and increasing profits) to their balance sheet (increasing assets).

One month after disclosing the misstatement of earnings, WorldCom was forced to file the largest bankruptcy in corporate history. Thousands of employees lost their jobs. Stock that was once worth $64 a share became worthless. Thousands of shareholders lost their total investment. Several executives, including the CEO, CFO, controller, and some mid-level employees, went to prison.

In another case, Enron, with 22,000 employees and annual revenues exceeding $100 billion, collapsed in just a few months in late 2001 after it was disclosed that it had hidden loans in excess of $6 billion which had been kept off its balance sheet. Again, thousands of employees lost their jobs and savings. Twenty-three individuals pleaded guilty to criminal charges. CEO Kenneth Lay and COO Jeffery Skilling were tried and convicted of several counts of fraud. Skilling was sentenced to twenty-four years in prison. Lay died before his sentence went into effect.[12]

On March 12, 2009, Bernard Madoff, long-time Wall Street investment advisor, pleaded guilty to criminal charges for a Ponzi-like scheme that defrauded investors of billions of dollars. The size of the amounts missing from client accounts and fabricated gains was unprecedented, totaling $64 billion. Madoff, who was seventy-one, was sentenced to 150 years in prison. [13]

The human toll from these three illustrations of business and investment fraud is incalculable. In addition to the thousands of jobs lost and life savings wiped out, many personal lives were shattered, including the spouses and children of those found guilty and sentenced to prison. One of Madoff's sons committed suicide. Trust in our business, accounting, and investment institutions has been gravely weakened. Isaiah summed all of this up well when he said, "Woe to those who call evil good and good evil, and darkness for light and light for darkness" (Is 5:20).

In spite of the many problems that we see in the workplace and in our culture at large, the good news is that God has a response for these problems. He is available to each of us and can show us how to deal with such problems so that our lives are transformed and so that we, in partnership with him, can transform the workplace around us.

Questions for Reflection or Discussion

1. In your workplace, do you serve your employer, customers, colleagues, subordinates—or yourself? When facing a task, who do you think of first?

2. How would you rank your work in the priorities of your life?

3. How often do you miss dinner with your family due to work commitments?

4. How do you cope with an ever-increasing workload?

5. What action would you take if your company or boss is seeking to do something you believe to be unethical?

6. How have you responded to temptations to misreport something for which you are responsible—progress reports, expense accounts, accounting entries, performance appraisals, etc.?

7. How do you measure your success? Is it by position, salary level, recognition, service to employer or others, or by whether you are fulfilling God's will?

8. Does your belief in God impact your work and workplace environment? Have you compartmentalized your life, keeping your faith separated from your work?

Chapter Two

CHRIST IN YOU:
PART OF GOD'S PLAN

God's plan for his creation is to dwell in us, his human creatures, through his son, Jesus Christ, so that we, with the power of the Holy Spirit, can partner with God in bringing his presence to the people and circumstances of our lives. Sadly, many Christians do not recognize that God dwells in them. They do not appropriate the power of the Holy Spirit that is in them through their baptism. They are unaware that the living God is present in them and desires to work through them in their individual situations.

In ancient times God spoke through the prophets to bring his presence to people and to teach them his ways and show them how to live. In Jesus, God demonstrated his great love and mercy for us by becoming one of us to bring his presence into the world in a very concrete way at a specific moment and time in history. Jesus demonstrated his great love and mercy for us by sacrificing his life to free us from the grip of sin and Satan's power over the world. By the resurrection of Jesus, God confirmed the saving nature and power of that sacrifice. St. Paul summarized it this way:

"In the past God spoke to our forefathers through the prophets at many times and in various ways, but in these last days he has spoken to us by his Son, whom he appointed heir of all things, and through whom he made the universe. The Son is the radiance of God's glory and the exact representation of his being, sustaining all things by his powerful word" (Heb 1:1-3).

Through Jesus, God invites us to have a personal relationship with him. The Gospel of John declares, "Yet to all who received him, to those who believed in his name, he gave the right to become children of God—children born not of natural descent, nor of human decision or a husband's will, but born of God" (Jn 1:12-13). Thus, we who are made in the image and likeness of God become children of God when we receive Jesus Christ and believe in his name.

Dwelling in Us

Jesus says, "Here I am! I stand at the door and knock. If anyone hears my voice and opens the door, I will come in and eat with him, and he with me" (Rev 3:20). Jesus wants to be a part of your life. He wants to be your friend. He wants to have an ongoing, two-way conversation with you, the more intimate the better. He wants to dwell in you, so he can go where you go, say what you say, do what you do, be what you can be. The more you open the door to him, the more you are aware of him dwelling in you 24/7, the more you can reflect his presence and power in your life to impact the people and circumstances around you. His presence will transform your life and enable you to influence others and the environments in which you live and work.

After I experienced Jesus in a new way, he gave me an intense desire to spend time with him and to read his Word. Previously, I would pray at Mass, say grace at meals, and perhaps offer up a prayer when facing some challenge, but prayer was not a regular part of my life. I seldom read the Bible. After my encounter with Jesus, however, I *wanted* to read the Bible. Sometimes the words seemed to leap off the page, as God gave me new meaning and insights I had never seen before.

While my prayer life was initially spotty, eventually I came to realize that the only way I could satisfy the desire to be with Jesus was to get up earlier each morning and devote a period of time to him before breakfast and leaving for work. This has become my "appointment with God." We regularly make appointments in our work. We make appointments with doctors, with our children's teachers and with friends for social occasions. Why not with Jesus?

Any relationship—be it with a spouse, a friend, or one of our children—cannot develop and grow without time spent together. Our relationship with God is no different. Our salvation is dependent on our acceptance of God's offer of friendship.

William A. Barry, SJ, in his book, *A Friendship Like No Other,* says, "From the beginning of human existence on earth, God's plan for the world has entailed human acceptance of God's friendship. We turned away from friendship and lost our way. God's answer was to renew the offer of friendship and to send the Son to share our lot and show us how to live as friends of God. Thus, the saving of the world comes about heart by heart, as it were. God offers friendship to each human being not only as a path for his or her salvation but also as a means to the salvation of the world."[1] The furtherance of God's kingdom on this earth is dependent upon our letting God dwell in us so that we can cooperate with him in fulfilling his will for us and becoming "partners with God in the family business."

This is what Jesus intended when he said, "Before long, the world will not see me anymore, but you will see me. Because I live, you also will live. On that day you will realize that I am in my Father and you are in me, and I am in you" (Jn 14:19-20). A couple of verses later Jesus says that he and the Father "will make our home in you" (Jn 14:23). Years later John commented in one of his letters, "We can know that we are living in him and he is living in us because he lets us share his Spirit" (1Jn 4:13). Similarly, "Those who obey his commands live in him and he in them. And this is how we know that he lives in us: We know it by the Spirit he gave us" (1 Jn 3:24). Finally, Peter boldly proclaims that we "share the divine nature" (2 Pt 1:4).

Christians throughout the ages have witnessed to this reality. One of the early Church fathers, Cyril of Jerusalem, says, "You who are sharers of Christ through baptism, are appropriately called, Christs."[2] St. Augustine proclaims, "Let us rejoice and give thanks; we have not only become Christians, but Christ himself…. Stand in awe and rejoice, we have become Christ."[3] At the time of the Reformation, Martin Luther proclaimed, "In faith itself Christ is really present."[4]

Today, both Catholic and Protestant voices witness to this reality. The *Catechism of the Catholic Church*, in linked passages from Scripture and Tradition, says, "The Word became flesh to make us partakers of the divine nature: For this is why the Word became man, and the Son of God became the Son of man: so that man, by entering into communion with the Word and thus receiving divine sonship, might become a son of God."[5]

Anglican biblical scholar, N. T. Wright, in his book, *The New Testament and the People of God*, says:

"Reality as we know it is the result of a creator god bringing into being a world that is other than himself, and yet which is full of his glory. It was always the intention of this god that creation should one day be flooded with his own life, in a way for which it was prepared from the beginning. As a part of a means to this end, the creator brought into being a creature which, by bearing the creator's image, would bring his wise and loving care to bear upon creation. By a tragic irony, the creature in question has rebelled against this intention. But the creator has solved this problem in principle in an entirely appropriate way, and as a result is now moving the creation once more towards its originally intended goal. The implementation of this solution now involves the indwelling of this god with his human creatures and ultimately within the whole creation, transforming it into that which was made in the beginning."[6]

A Personal Pentecost

Why is it that many Christians today do not experience the reality of Christ alive in them? Why don't more of us experience Christ present and acting in us through the power of the Holy Spirit which we received in baptism? The answer is found in the individual choices we make that determine whether God is buried alive or made alive in each of us. Do we bury God's presence in us, hiding him—or do we let him be seen, heard, and experienced?

I lived my life for years in a way that buried God's presence in me rather than allow that presence to be manifested. I believed in God, attended Mass regularly, and participated in the sacraments. Yet my Christian faith had become secondary to other so-called priorities, namely my career. I didn't recognize God's presence in my life, and no one else did either.

Because I had compartmentalized my life, the blessings of Christ's truth, compassion, and healing power were not available to the area of my life that needed them most—my work life. I put Jesus in a box. I left him in the parking lot and went into my office. I separated my business and professional life from the reality of Christ's presence in me.

When I met Jesus Christ and asked him to take the disorder and sin in my life, that all changed. Some people subsequently prayed with me for the release of the power of the Holy Spirit, and I began to experience the presence of God and the fullness of the Holy Spirit in a new and deeper way. I experienced a renewal of my faith.

Kevin and Dorothy Ranaghan explain in their book, *Catholic Pentecostals*, that praying for the release of the power of the Holy Spirit "is a prayer for renewal for everything that Christian initiation is meant to be." This "is neither a new sacrament nor a substitute sacrament. Like the renewal of baptismal promises, it is a renewal in faith of the desire to be everything that Christ wants us to be."[7] The sacrament of baptism that I experienced in my youth, which I had allowed to become dormant, was now actualized. If you ask my wife, she will tell you that from that day forward my perspective, focus, and priorities began to change. The words of Jesus to the disciples in the Book of Acts and the description of the coming of the Holy Spirit on the first Christians became real to me.

In Acts, Jesus told the disciples not to leave Jerusalem, but to "wait for the gift my Father promised, which you have heard me speak about. For John baptized with water, but in a few days you will be baptized with the Holy Spirit.... You will receive power when the Holy Spirit comes on you; and you will be my witnesses in Jerusalem and in all Judea and Samaria, and to the ends of the earth" (Acts 1:4-5, 8). Luke later reports that on the day of Pentecost they were all gathered together in one place when "suddenly a sound like the blowing of a violent wind came from heaven and filled the whole house…. They saw what seemed to be tongues of fire that separated and came to rest on each of them. All of them were filled with the Holy Spirit and began to speak in other tongues as the Spirit enabled them" (Acts 2:2-4).

When the bystanders did not understand what was happening, Peter stood up to explain that God was pouring out his Spirit on all people as had been foretold by the prophet Joel (see Jl 2:28-32), just as Jesus had said. Peter exhorted everyone: "Repent and be baptized in the name of Jesus Christ for the forgiveness of your sins. And you will receive the gift of the Holy Spirit. The promise is for you and your children and for all who are far off… for all whom the Lord our God will call" (Acts 2:38-39).

This promise is for each of us. The same Holy Spirit that Jesus said would empower the disciples to be his witnesses throughout the earth is waiting to be released in you to renew your faith, to draw you into a closer relationship with the Father, and to build God's kingdom in the circumstances of your life, including your workplace.

This is not just about learning biblical principles and applying them to workplace problems. While Scripture certainly assists us in coming to know God, this is about *being*. It is about the presence of God dwelling in you and allowing the Holy Spirit to open your eyes, mind, and heart to God's Word, ways, and will. It is about being one with Jesus and the Father. It's about being Christ through the power of the Holy Spirit to the people and circumstances in your life.

Blessed John Paul II characterized the role of the Holy Spirit as follows:

> "The Holy Spirit 'anoints' the baptized, sealing each with an indelible character (2 Cor 1:21-22), and constituting each as a spiritual temple with the Holy presence of God as a result of each person's being united and likened to Jesus Christ. With this spiritual 'unction' Christians can repeat in an individual way the words of Jesus: 'The Spirit of the Lord is upon me, because he has anointed me to preach the good news to the poor. He has sent me to proclaim release to the captives and recovery of sight to the blind, to set at liberty those who are oppressed, to proclaim the acceptable year of the Lord' (Lk 4:18-19; Is. 61:1-2). Thus, with the outpouring of the Holy Spirit in Baptism and Confirmation, the baptized share in the same mission of Jesus as the Christ, the Savior-Messiah."[8]

Acting in and with the Spirit

In Christ, we are united with God. We become his body and his hands working in the world. God operates in us and with us, and we can bring his presence and power into the daily circumstances of our lives.

Beverly Blount is a chemotherapy nurse for an oncology clinic in Gilroy, California. She says, "When patients first come in, they are scared. We talk to them, make them feel welcome, give them a hug, and assure them that they will be fine. When I start an IV, I say, 'Let's pray that this IV will be painless.' They start to relax. At some point I will ask the patient if I can pray with him or her. They always say okay."

Beverly, who is also a noted Gospel singer and concert violinist, will sometimes sing or play the violin for patients. One patient said, "Beverly sings and dances; she's comic relief. She sang 'I Believe I Can Fly' for me, and she will sing at my memorial service and play 'Ave Maria' on the violin."

"We get very close to many of our patients," Beverly says. "I went to Pat's house to help her out before she died. We'll go to the hospital and pray with patients, even in a coma. People tell me, 'You shouldn't get so close to your patients,' but I tell them that this is my 'God job.'"

Beverly brings God's presence to the patients that come to her clinic. She cares for them, she intercedes in prayer for them, she sings for them—she loves them just as Jesus would love them if he were physically present. The Holy Spirit in Beverly and her response enables this to happen.

God calls each of us to be Christ through the power of his Holy Spirit and to bring the presence of Christ to the people and circumstances of our lives. This is exactly what Paul was talking about when he said, "I have been crucified with Christ and I no longer live, but Christ lives in me" (Gal 2:20). He is describing the dramatic change he experienced through the power of the Holy Spirit. Christ was actually alive in him, working and doing the Father's will.

As the presence of Christ was in St. Paul, so also is the presence of Christ in Beverly, doing the Father's will and bringing the presence of God to the chemotherapy patients that come to her clinic.

Fully Equipped

God equips his people for the mission to which they are called. He promises us the power to do what Jesus did. Jesus said, "I tell you the truth, anyone who has faith in me will do what

I have been doing. He will do even greater things than these because I am going to the Father. And I will do whatever you ask in my name, so that the Son may bring glory to the Father" (Jn 14:12). Amazing! Jesus wants us to do the things he did in order to bring glory to the Father, and he empowers us to do so!

By the gifts of the Holy Spirit described in Isaiah 11:2-3 (wisdom, understanding, counsel, fortitude, knowledge, piety, and fear of the Lord) and the spiritual gifts described in 1 Corinthians 12:7-11 (wisdom, knowledge, faith, healing, miraculous powers, prophecy, discerning spirits, and speaking in tongues), God equips us to do all that he asks of us as we carry out his will.

A few years ago, my wife and I were at a reception to celebrate my retirement from Mobil. As we stood in a certain spot, various colleagues and friends came by to visit and wish us well.

A woman named Ann extended her best wishes and then said, "You know my son is now sixteen years old." I apparently gave her a blank stare, not reacting to what she had said.

"Don't you remember our conversation in your office that day?" she asked. Her eyes started to well up with tears as she said, "My son would probably not be here if it were not for the conversation we had." I did remember and gave her a big hug.

Seventeen years earlier, Ann was going to have an abortion and she told my secretary, who came to me and asked me to talk with her. I responded that I would be happy to talk with Ann if she wanted to talk with me. Later, Ann came to speak with me. She was one of our legal department's word processors back in the days before a personal computer was on everyone's desk. She was a couple of years out of high school, had become pregnant, and the prospective father refused to take any responsibility. She had little family or support in the area and didn't think she could be a mother.

I don't remember all that was said, but we talked for a long time about how she was carrying a real person inside her and how God had already given that little person a soul and an identity. We talked, she cried, and we prayed. I remember praying with her that God would show her love and give her wisdom and courage. A few weeks later, Ann decided not to have an abortion, and later she decided to raise the baby herself as a single mother.

Back at the retirement reception, standing next to Ann was one of Mobil's executive vice presidents. He had a reputation for being a tough senior executive and had given me my share of difficult moments over the years. As Ann was retelling her story, I noticed a tear trickling down the side of his face, and I could tell he was visibly moved. In fact, we were all a bit teary-eyed before Ann finished.

Over the course of my last week at Mobil, I was the beneficiary of many kind words, courtesies, and gifts, but the greatest honor and gift was being reminded of that conversation with Ann. While I may have not realized it at the time, God was working through me to bring his love and support to Ann. Several gifts of the Holy Spirit were in play—wisdom, knowledge, faith, healing, and prophecy. I wasn't thinking about them. They were just present to Ann through me. As a result, one life was changed—Ann's—and another life was allowed to live—her son's.

Just as God became flesh in Jesus through the power of the Holy Spirit in Mary, he later became flesh in the apostles through the same Holy Spirit. Today, he can become flesh in us when we repent of our sins, accept his offer to dwell in us, and seek the release of the power of the Holy Spirit. Pentecost is the natural follow-on to Christmas and Easter in completing God's incarnation in us, which leads to his ultimate objective of filling the world with his presence. When that happens, God's gifts become our gifts. His strength becomes our strength. His Word becomes our word. His love, which St. Paul declares is the greatest of all gifts, becomes our love.

Through the gift of wisdom, we begin to understand the world around us from God's perspective instead of the world's conventional thinking. We begin to recognize sin more readily and the deceptive forms of temptation. Our discernment of the presence of good and evil is enhanced. St. Paul describes this as a part of taking on "the mind of Christ" (1 Cor 2:16).

Healing and Miracles

The gift of healing and miracles were not meant only for the early Church, but also for us in our day as well. I have personally experienced physical healing through prayer and the power of the Holy Spirit in my own life and in the life of my children. After being diagnosed with glaucoma and the loss of about 30 percent of my field of vision, some friends prayed with me for healing. At my next appointment, my ophthalmologist was surprised to discover that my field of vision had been restored 100 percent. When I reminded him that he had previously told me that the vision which was lost could never be restored, and that some people had prayed with me for healing, he said, "I will take all the help I can get."

Our daughter, Emily, was born with Down syndrome and a heart condition known as "A-V Canal," which involves holes between her auricles and ventricles. The hole between her ventricles was particularly serious and required surgery when she was five months old. Three different cardiologists confirmed this diagnosis and treatment. On the weekend before her scheduled surgery, friends came to our house to pray with Emily for healing. A few days later, at her pre-surgical catheterization, the critical hole between her ventricles was no longer present, and the surgery was cancelled. The surgery to correct the hole between her auricles was put off until she was four years old when she was much bigger and stronger.

The Holy Spirit gives us the strength to do what we could never do on our own. When we first learned that Emily was born with Down syndrome, I was shocked, filled with sorrow and fear. I knew nothing about Down syndrome children, so I thought only the worst. On the second evening after she was born, I cried out to the Lord for understanding and asked him to take the anguish I was experiencing.

He responded. He calmed my fears. He gave me peace. He started to share his mind with me about his love for his special children—children who never offend him as the rest of us do, who never pervert the work of his hands, who have no guile but only purity of heart. Through the power of the Holy Spirit, God opened my mind to see Emily as he sees her. His strength became my strength. When I look back today and see the joy, love, and understanding that Emily has brought to Marilynn and me, our children, and all who have encountered her, I have only praise and thanksgiving in my heart for God and all that he has done.

Through the power of the Holy Spirit, God's love becomes our love. Jesus says, "My command is this: Love each other as I have loved you. Greater love has no one than this, that he lay down his life for his friends" (Jn 15:12-13). A few years ago, I was diagnosed with a fairly advanced and aggressive form of prostate cancer. I have never experienced God's love more than I did in the months before and after my surgery and subsequent therapy—a love manifested by the prayer, fasting, and countless expressions and actions of love from my wife, children, neighbors, friends, former colleagues at Mobil, along with my brothers and sisters in Christians in Commerce and the Christian community to which we belong.

Let me share just a couple of examples. One of the first people to come and see me after my diagnosis was a close Christian brother who I had known for twenty-five years. He had been suffering from renal cell carcinoma, had endured surgery to remove one of his kidneys, and underwent various regimens of chemotherapy and radiation. He also had considerable difficulty walking due to neuropathy in his feet. At the time I was working in the Christians in Commerce offices, which are located on the second floor of an old, two-story building in Falls Church, Virginia. As I was sitting in my office, I heard a knock on the back door, and to my surprise, there was Dave. What is remarkable about this is that to get to our offices he had to walk up a steep, open steel stairway at the back of the building, more like a fire escape than a stairway. There stood Dave with his cane, notwithstanding all of the pain and difficulties he experienced in walking. Instead of just calling me on the phone, he was determined to come and personally encourage and assure me with respect to my anxiety over one aspect of my upcoming treatment. I would have never expected him to walk up that difficult stairway, but his love for me overrode his physical difficulties.

Ten days prior to my surgery, I attended a scheduled board meeting of Christians in Commerce in Phoenix, Arizona. The board members decided that they would fast for me from Thursday evening to Friday evening and then conclude the fast by inviting members of the local Christians in Commerce chapters to join them in praying over me that Friday evening. I was overwhelmed by the number of people who took time out of their weekend schedule to show up on a Friday evening and pray.

Praying with Others

"Love each other as I have loved you," Jesus says in John 15:12. When you read this verse, you may tend to think of it as applying to someone who is close to you, such as a spouse, family member, or Christian friend, but it is also meant for your colleagues in the workplace. Yes, you are to love them as well. The context may be different, but the command remains the same. Love in the workplace means respecting the dignity of every individual, valuing each person's contribution, and dealing truthfully with subordinates, customers, and shareholders. It includes listening and sometimes, if the opportunity arises, sharing our Christian faith. It includes intercessory prayer for the good of your employer and the needs of others. Sometimes, it includes prayer on the spot with someone if that is what the Spirit calls you to do.

Jack McCall is a business insurance broker in San Jose, California. He often finds himself in situations where a customer, colleague, or even a stranger may have a need that results in Jack praying with them. Jack says, "Praying with another person has become one of the most intimate gifts of God for me. I find myself asking God for permission to pray with another person the way he would."

"One of my customers called and shared that he would be closing his business and asked me to cancel all of his insurance policies. 'I can do that,' I said. 'Are you retiring?' He said, 'Yes,

I have Parkinson's.' I said, 'How's your relationship with God?' There was silence. So, I began to pray for him over the phone. It was something God wanted me to do for this man."

In another story, Jack reports, "A man in a deep depression called me for help. I knew by the sound of his voice that this was not going to be a quick-fix situation—this was about saving his life. He refused to seek professional help, so I told him I'd call him every day at a certain time until he was out of the woods. We talked daily and became very close on the phone, and we always ended our time with prayer. If you asked him today, he would say I saved his life, but we know who really saved it. As God loved him through me, I was also being loved by God through him. We talk about once a month now."

Sometimes Jack prays with strangers. "One day I ran down to a coffee shop near my office to get a cup of coffee. A woman approached me saying, 'The waitresses here said I should have you remember my daughter-in-law, Terri, in your prayers. She is in the hospital with a virus in her lungs. The doctors don't know what it is.' I said, 'Instead of remembering her later, why not pray for her right now?' She looked at me with a look of shock in her eyes, as if to say, 'Here?' We did pray for Terri, and it was good. Did God hear our prayer? Yes! Who was affected most by the prayer? We were all blessed. Crying, she kissed me on the cheek and smiled at me like we were the only ones in the coffee shop."

Jack brought God's love and healing to each of these people. He allowed God to work through him by the power of the Holy Spirit. Several gifts of the Holy Spirit were active in Jack: wisdom, faith, discerning of spirits, healing, prophecy, and above all, love. Jack's love of God and compassion overcame any anxiety involving the risks of rejection and ridicule.

Experiencing the Power of the Holy Spirit

How can you experience the power of the Holy Spirit? Simply ask for it. Jesus said, "So I say to you: Ask and it will be given to you; seek and you will find; knock and the door will be opened to you. For everyone who asks receives; he who seeks finds; and to him who knocks, the door will be opened" (Lk 11:9). Jesus then uses the analogy of how parents know how to give good gifts to their children by saying, "If you then, though you are evil, know how to give good gifts to your children, how much more will your Father in heaven give the Holy Spirit to those who ask him" (Lk 11:13).

We are not talking about a new or substitute sacrament here, but the renewal of our faith in Jesus and the Holy Spirit that we received in baptism. This is about experiencing Jesus and the Holy Spirit in line with what was promised in the Gospels, similar to what the early Christians experienced in the Book of Acts and what St. Paul describes in his letters as Christ being alive in him. This is all meant to enable us to do the things that Jesus did to bring about the kingdom of God on this earth in our time and place.

Although many experience this release of the power of the Holy Spirit through the prayer of others praying with them, no special ritual or formula is required. God can act in the life of anyone who seeks him humbly and sincerely.

The ministry of Christians in Commerce provides an opportunity through its Challenge Weekends for people to get away from their normal routines for a weekend to take stock of their lives, repent of any sin, commit or recommit their lives to Jesus Christ, and be prayed with for the baptism in the Holy Spirit. This takes place simply by other Christian business people who are present praying in a small group for each individual. They usually put a hand on the person's shoulder and pray for the release of the power and the gifts of the Holy Spirit in his or her life. If God is calling us to build his kingdom and make a difference in the world around us, he is going to equip us to get the job done.

Brothers in Christ

John DeSanto was a county prosecutor in Duluth, Minnesota, for many years. In one of his first cases, as he looked across the counsel table at the defendant, he was surprised to see Jim, someone from his high school. This was not the last time that John would see Jim across the counsel table. Over the next twenty-six years, John would prosecute Jim a dozen times for theft-related crimes to support his chemical dependency. He became well known to the entire criminal justice system as he continued to commit crimes, get caught, go to prison, get out, commit more crimes, get caught again, and go back to prison over and over again.

During the first few prosecutions, John thought the same— that Jim was just another hopeless criminal. Then John recommitted his life to Jesus Christ and received the baptism in the Holy Spirit. The next time he saw Jim in court, he told him that he was praying for him as Jim went back to prison. At first Jim would say, "John, don't waste your time." In subsequent cases, Jim started to thank John for his prayers and said that he would in turn pray for John.

Then Jim was again caught with a large cache of stolen goods, pleaded guilty, and was on his way back to prison. While awaiting sentencing, Jim learned that he was terminally ill with sclerosis of the liver. His lawyer persuaded the judge to let him die in a hospice outside of prison. Jim also asked his lawyer to request that John would pray for him.

Over the next six months, John did more than just pray for Jim. He visited him two to four times a week at various hospice units. They reminisced about growing up in the 1950s and talked about their favorite baseball teams and players. They also read the Bible together. That fall, Jim repented of his sins and surrendered his life to Jesus Christ. He died in late November.

"Over those last six months, I frequently called Jim 'brother' because we were brothers in Christ," said John. "Jim loved reading and praying the psalms. We read them many times together, and they have new meaning to me now. God used Jim to teach me about acceptance of suffering and perseverance, and he showed me that it's never too late to say yes to the Lord, no matter what we have done in the past."

John concludes, "Because God answers payers, Jim said 'yes' to Christ before he died, and I know he is in paradise today—just like another thief who died on the cross next to Jesus 2,000 years ago."

John's story speaks for itself, but there are a few lessons in it for all of us.

- We can't share Christ with someone unless we have experienced him ourselves. Notice the difference in John's attitude before and after he surrendered his life to Christ and experienced the baptism in the Holy Spirit. Moreover, he had great compassion for Jim and was willing to share his time with Jim, not just once but several times a week for over six months, in order to support Jim and gently lead him to Christ. John was exhibiting the fruit of the Spirit described by St. Paul in Galatians 5:22-23: "love, joy, peace, patience, kindness, goodness, faithfulness, gentleness, and self-control."

• John experienced a renewal of his Christian faith when he recommitted his life to Christ and experienced the release of the power of the Holy Spirit. It made a difference in his life, how he perceived and conducted his job, and how he related to people. John, who is now a state court judge, considered his job as a criminal prosecutor a God-given vocation. He believes that God put him in his job and gave him the skills to do it well so he could be the presence of Christ to both the victims of crimes and the people he prosecuted. Before every trial John says, "I pray for the truth to be known, for a just result, and that everyone involved would come to know Christ."

God desires that we experience renewal in our lives, come to know him more deeply, build an ongoing relationship with him, and allow him to work through us by the power of the Holy Spirit. How do we experience God in this way? Simply ask for it.

Questions for Reflection or Discussion

1. What is the nature of your relationship with God and his son, Jesus Christ? Is it distant, with God "up there" and "you down here?" Is it emergency related, where you call upon him only in time of trouble? Is it casual—on-again, off-again? Or is it a friendship with regular communication?

2. Read Revelation 3:19-22 and John 1:12-13; 14:15-24; and 15:14-15. Do you believe God desires to dwell in you? If so, how have you experienced his presence?

3. Have you experienced the presence and power of the Holy Spirit in your life as described in chapters 2 and 3 of the Book of Acts? If so, how has it made a difference in your life? If not, simply ask

God to forgive you for any sin in your life, commit or recommit your life to Jesus Christ, and ask him to release the power of the Holy Spirit in you.

4. Have you experienced any of the gifts of the Holy Spirit as described in Isaiah 11:2-3 and 1 Corinthians 12:7-11 (wisdom, understanding, counsel, fortitude, knowledge, piety, fear of the Lord, faith, healing, miraculous powers, prophecy, discerning of spirits, and praying in tongues)? Reflecting on the stories in this chapter, think of ways the Holy Spirit has enabled you to serve others, including people in your workplace.

Chapter Three

WORK: PART
OF GOD'S DESIGN

Work is part of God's design for creation. God was the first to work in his act of creation. "By the seventh day God had finished the work he had been doing; so on the seventh day he rested from all of his work" (Gn 2:2). In creating us in his image and likeness, his intention was that we would cooperate with him "to work and take care of it [creation]" (Gn 2:15). It was intended to be a team effort—God and us working together for the advancement of the general welfare of creation. Jesus acknowledged this when he said, "My Father is always at work to this very day. and I, too, am working" (Jn 5:17).

The Importance of Work

The *Catechism of the Catholic Church* states, "Human work proceeds directly from persons created in the image of God and called to prolong the work of creation by subduing the earth, both with and for one another. Hence work is a duty: 'If any one will not work, let him not eat' (2 Thess 3:10). Work honors the Creator's gifts and the talents received from him. Work is for man, not man for work. Everyone should be able to draw from work the means of providing for his life and that of his family, and of serving the human community."[1] Stefan Cardinal Wyszynski, in his book *All You Who Labor*, says, "The summons to work on this earth is God's general mobilization."[2]

In Jesus' parable of the workers in the vineyard (see Mt 20:1-16), when the owner of the vineyard went out at the eleventh hour and found still others standing around, he asked, "Why have you been standing here all day long doing nothing?" When they replied that no one had hired them, he said, "You also go work in my vineyard." God, the owner of the vineyard, does not want us to sit around idle. He intends for us to work; work is a part of his plan.

Lester DeKoster, in his book, *Work, the Meaning of Your Life*, defines work as "the form in which we make ourselves useful to others and thus to God."[3] DeKoster explains, "Culture and civilization don't just happen. They are made to happen and keep happening—by God the Holy Spirit through our work."[4]

He poses the question of what would happen if everyone quit working, and answers, "Civilized life quickly melts away. Food vanishes from the store shelves, gas pumps dry up, streets are no longer patrolled, and fires burn themselves out. Communication and transportation services end and utilities go dead. Those who survive at all are soon huddled around campfires, sleeping in tents, and clothed in rags. The difference between barbarism and culture is, simply, work. As seeds multiply themselves into harvest, so work flowers into civilization."[5] By tending the garden of God's creation, our work leads to the development of civilization and the furtherance of God's creation to his intended purpose when he will one day be "be all in all" (1 Cor 15:28).

DeKoster supports his view of work by relying on the Parable of the Sheep and the Goats found in Matthew 25:31-46. In this parable Jesus says:

"When the Son of Man comes in his glory, and all of the angels with him, he will sit on his thrown in heavenly glory. All of the nations will be gathered before him, and he will separate the people one from another as a shepherd separates the sheep from the goats. He will put the sheep on his right and the goats on his left.

"Then the King will say to those on his right, 'Come, you who are blessed by my Father; take your inheritance, the kingdom prepared for you since the creation of the world. For I was hungry and you gave me something to eat, I was thirsty and you gave me something to drink, I was a stranger and you invited me in, I needed clothes and you clothed me, I was sick and you looked after me, I was in prison and you came to visit me.'

"Then the righteous will answer him, 'Lord, when did we see you hungry and feed you, or thirsty and give you something to drink? When did we see you a stranger and invite you in, or needing clothes and clothe you? When did we see you sick or in prison and go to visit you?'

"The King will reply, 'I tell you the truth, whatever you did for one of the least of these brothers of mine, you did for me.'

"The king then turns to those on his left and tells them to depart from him, for he was hungry and thirsty, a stranger and needed clothes, was sick and in prison, and they did not tend to him. Like those on his right, they answer, 'Lord, when did we see you hungry or thirsty or a stranger or needing clothes or sick or in prison, and did not help you?'

"He will reply, 'I tell you the truth, whatever you did not do for one of the least of these, you did not do for me.'

"Then they will go to eternal punishment but the righteous to eternal life."

While this parable is usually considered to be about the universal judgment of all people taking into account how they have loved and served others, DeKostner contends that Jesus is talking not only about those who are in need, but also about the basic needs of creation. He enlarges the perspective of providing food, drink, clothing, shelter, and healthcare to the basic necessities of life for all of humanity as represented by the many occupations that make up civilization. Farming, transportation, grocery stores, restaurants, public utilities, drilling, pipe-laying, plumbing, textiles, retailing, construction, medical services, health insurance, social services, education, communications… "The fabric of civilization, like all fabrics, is made up of countless tiny threads—each thread, the work of someone."[6]

All work that contributes to the production of goods or services for others, unless it is immoral, is part of God's plan for creation. As the parable says, our reward (inheriting the kingdom) was prepared for us "since the creation of the world." Thus, work has always been a part of God's plan and his intention for his creation. What surprises people in the parable is that in working at providing the basic necessities for others they are serving God himself.

Like the people in the parable, we may be surprised that in doing our work we, too, are serving God. Whether we are a migrant farm worker, a construction day laborer, an employee on a manufacturing assembly line, a public office holder, a professional athlete, a teacher, a stay-at-home parent, a doctor, or an executive for a large international corporation, our work is about taking care of the garden of creation. It is about advancing creation and the civilization that flows from it. Our work has dignity, intrinsic value, and purpose.

In his encyclical, *Laborem Exercens,* Blessed John Paul II says:

"The word of God's revelation is profoundly marked by the fundamental truth that man, created in the image of God, shares by his work in the activity of the Creator and that, within the limits of his own human capabilities, man in a sense continues to develop that activity, and perfect it as he advances further and further in the discovery of the resources and values contained in the whole of creation. For, while providing the substance of life for themselves and their families, men and women are performing their activities in a way which appropriately benefits society. They can justly consider that by their labor they are unfolding the Creator's work, and contributing to the realization in history of the divine plan."[7]

The truth that man participates in the activity of God through work was evident in Jesus' life, for he himself was a man of work. Jesus, a carpenter's son, likely spent much of his adult life as a carpenter until age thirty when he began his ministry.

Blessed John Paul II continues, "The eloquence of the life of Jesus Christ is unequivocal: he belongs to the 'working world', he has appreciation and respect for human work; he looks with love upon human work and the different forms that it takes."[8]

Look at how much work was connected to all Jesus said and did. Os Hillman, president of Marketplace Leaders Ministries, Inc., a Christian outreach to the workplace, offers the following observations about Jesus and work.

- Of Jesus' 132 public appearances in the New Testament, 122 were in the marketplace.

- Of the fifty-two parables Jesus told, forty-five had a workplace context.

- Jesus called twelve workplace individuals, not clergy, to build his church.[9]

Jesus' proclamation about the coming of the kingdom of God included many references to the workplace—farming, winemaking, raising sheep, banking and investing, house building, the practices of medicine and law, fishing, teaching, cooking, baking, real estate, government administration, and the military. His teaching and call to us apply to the whole of our lives, not just the spiritual. To be sure, belief in him and the Father, surrendering our lives to him and seeking his will in all things is paramount in his call, but this call is in the context of real life. Much of real life takes place in the workplace.

Working for God

After working in the Internet technical support industry for many years, Nancy Corbridge from Morgan Hill, California, decided that she wanted to do something different—"to work for God." She had grown weary of the bickering and conflicts that she had seen between management and employees and also between the employees themselves. She resigned from the Internet company and trained as a volunteer in a pregnancy care center, subsequently becoming its executive director.

"It is a wonderful job," said Nancy. "Much of my work is associating with churches of various denominations and asking them to partner with the pregnancy care center and join in our work. I also get involved in client counseling. Our task is to determine the needs of each of the clients and review all of the options available to them. We also get into lifestyle issues that contribute to the circumstances that give rise to their need to come to us. We respect their freedom, however, and they make the decision that they think best.

"We don't always get to see the results. Sometimes all we

can do is plant seeds. Once I had counseled a young, seventeen-year-old girl. I didn't know what she had decided to do until she walked into my office one year and four days later to show off her baby.

"When I first took this job, I thought I was leaving my prior employment to 'go work for God' because of the ministry-related nature of the job in working with various churches and counseling people who were making significant decisions about life.

"Upon further reflection, however, I remember that when employees with my prior employer were chastised or unfairly attacked by the owner of the company, they often came to me to talk. I would always tell them that I would be praying for them. Although at the time, I did not necessarily see this as 'working for God,' I guess it was 'going about my Father's business.'

"Previously, I always saw 'working for God' as being in an environment like a church or something labeled as a ministry, yet everything we do is 'God's work' whether we are working in a secular environment or in an environment like the pregnancy care center where we can freely pray with others, talk about the Lord, and share Scripture throughout the day. Now I see that no matter what we do, we can be partnering with God and bringing his presence to wherever we are, be it secular or ministry."

Over the past century, there has been a trend to secularize work—to separate it from faith. Our culture encourages this. As we have removed faith from our public schools and the public square, so too have we removed faith from the workplace. Separating our work from our faith was never a part of God's intention or plan. We still need faith. We still need surrender. We still need baptism. We still need the Church. But compartmentalizing our faith from our work puts God in a box, creating an artificial divide between faith and work, and faith and the advance of civilization. We limit God when we confine his presence to church or activities outside our work life. For most people, work comprises as much as 50 percent or more of their waking hours. Doug Sherman and William Hendricks, authors of *Your Work Matters to God*, said, "As Christians we have over many years allowed a chasm to grow between our faith and our day-to-day work, a chasm that God never intended."[10]

Job, Idol, or Partnership?

If we acknowledge that work is part of God's plan for us, how do we view our work? Do we look on it just as a job? Do we make it an idol, or do we see it as a call in partnership with God and his desire for us? Looking at work as a job takes on a pocketbook perspective. We work only to make a living. Work is a curse. Whether work has intrinsic value or serves others is irrelevant from the job perspective. We focus on how much money we can make so that we can do or have all the other things we want. We don't see it as a "thread in the larger fabric of civilization." The weakness in viewing work from a job perspective is that we tend to under invest by not giving work our best effort. It is simply a means to an end.

A second perspective is to make work an idol. Our work becomes an obsession, subordinating other responsibilities in our lives. That is what I did when I was a young attorney for Mobil. My focus was on my accomplishments so I could move up the corporate ladder. It became an obsession that often resulted in shortchanging my family and other important responsibilities. This kind of focus tends to be rather self-centered. If we can find a position that advances our career or where we can be "more fulfilled," then that is what we will do, regardless of the impact on other areas of our lives or what God's will may be for us. Here the vulnerability is to over-invest in work at the expense of our other responsibilities. There is a balance between good stewardship in striving for excellence in our work and maximizing the gifts and talents God has given us, and being obsessed with career advancement, reward, and personal fulfillment.

Finding the Balance

When I was in my mid-forties, I came face-to-face with this very issue. I was working for Mobil at its headquarters for the US Marketing and Refining Division in Fairfax, Virginia, when I was offered a new assignment to oversee the delivery of legal services for a major portion of Mobil's international marketing and refining operations. It was a great job and would have certainly furthered my career, but it required a move back to New York, where we had lived five years earlier.

We had three teenage daughters and a two-year-old son at the time. Our daughters were all doing well in school, were involved in Young Life (a Christian outreach to high school teenagers), and had great peers for friends. We had developed many close friends in our neighborhood, church, and community. We were concerned that we could not replicate these circumstances back in New York.

For three days, I agonized over the decision. While I didn't think I would be fired if I declined the assignment, I knew it would have a negative impact on my career. I talked with colleagues, my current boss, and his boss, who all stressed what a wonderful opportunity this would be. There was a lot of pressure to take the job and decide quickly since it would trigger many moves for other people. I prayed earnestly, asking the Lord what he wanted me to do. I consulted Christian friends, drew up lists of pros and cons, and talked at length with Marilynn. It was the most difficult decision I had ever faced.

Finally, we discerned that I should decline the offer. It did have a negative impact on my career for a number of years, but when I look back today and see all that has happened in the lives of our children and all the blessings we have experienced in our family, I am absolutely confident that this decision was God's will for us. Our children went on to complete their education and have since married wonderful Christians and are all raising Christian families.

Through this decision, God taught me that work is more than just a job, but it should not be treated as an idol. Rather, work is partnering with God, using the talents and gifts he has given us to serve others— all of which is part of a story much larger than ourselves. This is the kingdom perspective. Some call it a vocation. It has always been a part of God's plan that his human creation would partner with him in building his kingdom on earth. Work is faithful stewardship of our area of influence and authority entrusted into our care. Whatever our job and however it may be viewed, it has a value and is considered integral by God to the general welfare of the human race and the advancement of creation.

When asked what we do, most of us typically respond by saying what our occupation is. But we are really kingdom builders. What we do for a living may change, but our true call is to work in concert with God to establish his kingdom on earth. We do this by transforming where we work—offices, factories, farms, schools, services—into places that reflect the love of God, experience the power and presence of Christ, and produce goods and services with excellence. In fact, all men and women were created for this call, whether they acknowledge the Creator's existence or not.

Building the Kingdom

Kingdom building is a way of life; it should occupy a Christian's every waking moment. Kingdom building isn't about proselytizing our fellow workers or trying to make more money so that we can contribute additional sums to Christian ministry or causes. It isn't about creating "Christian businesses." While these things may result indirectly from our actions, kingdom building is about letting the presence of God in us be manifested in our daily decisions, in how we relate to others, and in being good stewards of all that God gives us. What we do, how we do it, and how it contributes to society are all part of bringing forth the kingdom of God. Jesus calls us to be the salt of the earth and the light of the world.

Barbara Grady, from Sacramento, California, worked in the juvenile court as a court clerk. While she was willing to witness to the Lord whenever she could, she found it hard. It was a very negative environment, not only due to the nature of cases and the people who appeared in court, but also with the court employees. "Part of my prayer on my way to work every day was to ask that others would see Christ and his love in me," said Barbara. "I wanted to love others as he loves. I invited people to my church and other Christian activities, and I shared stories about how God had helped me during tough times. I did not see any results, and I felt that God's presence in my life was not coming through."

When the court clerks' Christmas party came around, Barbara didn't want to go and kept making excuses. "My fellow clerks were very pushy about my attending," Barbara said. "Finally, one clerk whispered in my ear, 'You have to go. You have been elected Clerk of the Year.'"

At the presentation, Barbara learned to her surprise through the statements of her fellow clerks that Christ's presence in her had come through. Some of the things said were:

"I have never heard her say anything bad about anyone."

"I know better than to bad-mouth people around her. She just looks at me and I think, 'Oops! Can I reword that?'"

"I know if I need help with my work, she won't get mad or make me feel stupid."

"If you tell her something, it doesn't get spread all over Juvenile Hall."

"If I need advice, I know I can talk to her. She sees both sides and helps me see the other side too."

"I know she prays for me."

After listening to all of the comments, Barbara said, "I realized that my prayers had been answered, that sometimes people did see Christ in me, and that they did feel my love for them.

It is easy to let an office environment intimidate us, but Barbara relied on Jesus' promise to not be afraid because he would always be with her. Barbara was part of what God was doing at Juvenile Hall. She allowed Jesus to bring his love to the people there through her and show them how to relate to one another. She performed an important role in facilitating the care of juveniles in our system of justice, cooperating with God in bringing justice to his kingdom on earth.

We serve God when we view our work as a part of his kingdom and seek to do it with excellence. "Whatever you do, work at it with all your heart, as working for the Lord" (Col 3:23). Our work matters to God.

Questions for Reflection or Discussion

1. How do you view work? Do you think it matters to God? Do you consider it a part of God's plan for creation? Can you see it as a "thread in the larger fabric of civilization?"

2. Do you believe that you are serving God in your work? If so, how? If not, why not?

3. Do you view your work as a job—a means to an end so that you can have or do all the other things you want? Do you make it an idol, taking priority over all of the other responsibilities in your life? Do you see your work as a partnership with God?

4. Do you separate your faith from your work? Is your faith reflected in your conduct, how you relate to others and in your desire to do your work well?

Chapter Four

CHRIST WORKING THROUGH US

God's plan of working through us is a continuation of his incarnation begun in Jesus Christ and continued in us by the power of the Holy Spirit. St. Paul observes, "We are therefore Christ's ambassadors, as though God were making his appeal through us" (2 Cor 5:21). When we act on God's offer to dwell in us and conduct business with integrity, relate to employees, customers, suppliers, and colleagues with respect and seek excellence, in all that we do, we are partnering with God in advancing our piece of creation.

Integrity in Business Decisions and Practices

When God called Abraham and made a covenant with him to be his God and the God of his descendents for generations to come, he said, "Walk before me and be blameless" (Gn 17:1). God expected Abraham to live righteously in return for his covenant to establish a new people who would live under his care and provision. Similarly, he said to Solomon, "If you walk before me in integrity of heart and uprightness, as David your father did, and do all I command and observe my decrees and laws, I will establish your royal throne over Israel forever..." (1Kgs 9:4-5). Integrity encompasses many characteristics—honesty, honor, forthrightness, straightforwardness, perfection, wholeness, completeness, and purity, for example. We know that integrity is broken when we do not speak the truth, but it is also compromised when we embellish or stretch the truth, or when we gloss over problems and fail to mention unfavorable facts. However we might describe integrity, we seem to know it when we see it and when we don't, as the following stories will illustrate.

An Easy Choice

Bob Schumacher from San Jose, California, was in the highly competitive group insurance business for many years. A large produce company had asked Bob's firm to bid on a health insurance program for its union employees. As Bob analyzed the proposed program, he came to the conclusion that it was grossly inadequate in providing appropriate financial protection.

He and his partner were first tempted to propose a program that was within the budget being requested, since it would satisfy the cost requirements of both management and the union. At the presentation, however, Bob said, "The Spirit moved me to speak the truth. I told them that the current contract was twenty-five years behind the times in design and protection. It was inadequate, covering only small claims and leaving larger claims uncovered. I thought to myself, I am telling the owners and union representatives exactly what they *don't* want to hear. I told my partner we had a less than 5 percent chance of getting the business.

"Much to our surprise," Bob reported, "we were invited back to propose a program that had both the employer and the union employees agreeing to contribute more money to provide the protection they needed."

We see integrity in Bob's willingness to speak truthfully about the inadequacy of the customer's desired insurance program even at the risk of losing the business. His integrity was rewarded with getting the business and making the sale. This, however, is not always the result.

In another case, Bob was asked by the CFO of a family owned business with more than 100 employees to get a quote on tripling the life insurance coverage on all employees. It turned out that the husband of the CFO, who was also an employee, was seriously ill with cancer. The husband did not want his children, who were stockholders, to know that he had cancer. The CFO, who had been a customer of Bob's for over eight years, instructed him to keep the cancer confidential and not to disclose it to the insurance companies from whom he was getting quotes.

Bob told the CFO that he could not sign the application knowing that pertinent information was being withheld. As a result Bob's firm was dismissed. "It was a tough loss," Bob said. "We had served this company while it had grown from five employees to over 100. It resulted in a significant loss of income for our firm."

Three years after the CFO's husband died, the company asked Bob to bid on a benefits program once again. Bob's firm was one of four brokerage firms making recommendations. Surprisingly, all four firms made the same recommendations. The president of the company told the human resources director that it was an easy decision. As Bob relates, "The president said it was an easy decision because he knew he could trust our firm. We handled their insurance four more years until the company was purchased by Bechtel."

What Would Jesus Do?

Dick Kent once owned a large automotive repair facility in Falls Church, Virginia, that served both large commercial customers as well as retail consumers. He had just hired a new manager for one of his divisions. Dick recalls, "One day a vehicle was brought in for repair, an inspection was performed, and an estimate given which was approved by the customer. When the job was completed, we realized the customer was accidentally overcharged $400. The new manager came back into my office to ask what we should do—tell the customer or leave the bill as is, since the customer had approved the work being done for the original estimate."

"Frankly, I was dumbfounded," said Dick. "I asked him, 'If it were your mother's car that was in the shop for repairs, and the circumstances were the same, how would you want the shop to respond?' He lowered his head and said, 'Well, I'm sorry, but I haven't been here long, and I didn't know what kind of operation you ran here, Mr. Kent. Other places I have worked for would have simply said the job was approved at that amount so that is what they would charge.'

"As he was leaving my office, he repeated his apology and said, 'You know, I never even noticed the cross hanging there on your wall, but it explains a lot. As long as I'm here, Mr. Kent, questions like that will never need to be asked again.' Later that day I waited until the manager and I were alone. I told him of the short little phrase I try to remember to ask myself when I don't know which way to turn. It is simply, 'What would Jesus do?' When I eventually sold the business, almost eighteen years later, that same manager was still with me and we never had to experience a similar occurrence."

The Golden Rule

In another example of integrity, Leo Alonso, who runs a mortgage business in Silver Spring, Maryland, acted quite differently from what we read in the newspapers about all of the practices that gave rise to the subprime mortgage crisis. After real estate values escalated rapidly for several years, government-backed financial institutions began making loans available without requiring down payments or verification of earning capacity for certain categories of borrowers. When real estate values began to decline, then mortgage foreclosures began escalating at an alarming rate.

In the midst of all of this, Leo continued to conduct his mortgage brokerage business as he always had: with integrity and concern for the client foremost in his mind. "Most of our customers are Hispanic and first-time home buyers," says Leo. "They often need assistance in understanding the requirements and what is possible based upon their circumstances. Verification of earnings can be complicated because many of their employers pay them in cash. These are often people whose jobs include lawn work, house painting, and construction labor."

"In training our loan officers," Leo says, "our guiding principle is 'Do unto others as you would have them do unto you.' Their job isn't just to place loans. It is to assist people in doing what is right for them. I tell our loan officers to treat people as if they were brothers or sisters. The borrowers may not fully understand what they can do and how big a loan they can afford. It isn't unusual for our loan officers to counsel people to scale back from what they first desire because their financial situation will not support it.

"There are lots of opportunities for fraud in this business,"

Leo reports. "Clients will sometimes misstate their earnings, even submitting fake tax returns. For example, one person claimed to be a manager of a restaurant earning $100,000 a year when she was no longer employed. Some people will arrange for erroneous appraisals of property to justify the purchase price rather than basing it upon bona fide comparable sales. We lose a lot of loans because we will not go along with this and require full disclosure from the borrowers.

"In today's market, we spend our days trying to give advice on loan modifications, forbearance of loans, short sales, and deed in lieu of foreclosure cases. We receive no pay for this advice, but in the long run it will pay off. I tell our loan officers, 'Times are tough for many of our customers. Help them solve their problems. Treat them with dignity. They will know we care and they will come back to us and recommend new clients in the future.'

"From 1995 to 2008 we made more than 7,000 loans available to the Hispanic community. Before the real estate bubble, we were able to help many families get into first-time homes and start to build some wealth. Many bought homes for $80,000 to $130,000 that now are worth more than $400,000. This will be a legacy for their retirement years and an inheritance for their children."

If the entire mortgage industry had conducted business in a manner similar to Leo, it would be interesting to speculate whether the mortgage and financial crisis we have experienced in recent years would have been as severe as it has been. Our first reaction to such speculation might be that one person's example is not likely to impact an entire industry, but what if all of the many thousands of Christians who work in the financial and mortgage industry had let the Spirit of God lead them to conduct their work with the same integrity and concern for the customer as Leo? Would a different result have been possible? Isn't that what God is calling each of his followers to do?

A first cousin to integrity is God's call for us to be good stewards and to seek excellence in all that we do, as we learn how to let God work through us to build his kingdom in our place and time.

Seeking Excellence and Being Good Stewards

God expects us to be good stewards of his creation and to bear fruit with all that is entrusted to us. Jesus said, "You did not choose me, but I chose you and appointed you to go and bear fruit—fruit that will last" (Jn 15:16). We are expected to bear fruit with the time, talents, money, possessions, responsibilities, and people we have been given. Jesus illustrates this expectation with the Parable of the Talents (see Mt 25:14-30).

In this parable a man goes on a journey and entrusts his property to his servants, giving to one five talents of money, to another two talents, and to a third one talent, each according to his ability. The first at once put his money to work and gained five more talents. The second did the same and gained two more. But the man who was given one talent went off and dug a hole and hid his master's money. When the master returned from his journey, he asked for an accounting from his servants. The one who had been given five talents presented five more. His master said, "Well done, good and faithful servant! You have been faithful with a few things; I will put you in charge of many things." The second servant did the same and the master's reaction was the same. But the servant who had been given one talent said, "Master, I knew that you are a hard man, harvesting where you have not sown and gathering where you have not scattered seed. So I was afraid and went out and hid your talent in the ground. See, here is what belongs to you." The master's response was harsh, calling him a "wicked, lazy servant." He took the one talent from him and gave it to the one who had ten and instructed that this lazy servant be thrown outside into the darkness where there would be weeping and gnashing of teeth. This is one of Jesus' most severe responses to sinners and wrongdoing in the Bible.

Our purpose is not just to lead a godly life so we can go to heaven when we die. As the Parable of the Talents suggests, God also wants our lives and actions to yield an increase for his kingdom on earth here and now. He gives us talents that are often peculiar to our being and nature. He puts people in our lives and gives us responsibility for their care and welfare. This certainly includes our spouse and families, but it can also include employees in our workplace, or those for which we have a professional responsibility including clients, patients, students, and others. He gives us education and expertise to apply to the needs of society. How are we using these talents? How are we using our education and expertise? How are we caring for our spouse and children? How are we relating to colleagues? How are we carrying out our assigned job responsibilities?

In my last assignment with Mobil, I served as general manager of environmental, health, and safety. Shortly after assuming this job, I learned that I was expected to give a presentation to our executive committee and board of directors on the general state of the company's environmental, health, and safety performance.

In reviewing past reports to the board, I noticed that there had been no comparison of our company's performance in this area to our competitors' performance. We tracked competitive data relative to our financial performance in about every way in which it could be measured. Why weren't we doing the same in environment, health, and safety? So I asked our staff to gather information on our competitors' performance. It turned out that while we were doing well in several areas such as air emissions and spills, we were in seventh place out of the then eight major international oil companies with respect to employee safety and lost time accidents.

When others learned that we were going to report these competitive findings to the board, we started to get pushback from some quarters. One manager even threatened that if we did this there would be "blood on the floor"—*my* blood. This of course gave me pause, but my responsibility was to support the company's operations in improving its environmental, health, and safety performance. I wasn't sure that our executive committee really knew the truth of our safety performance compared to our competitors. If they knew the truth, I was certain they would want to do something about it.

We gave our report, first to the executive committee and then to the board. There was no "blood on the floor." Instead, the chairman looked around the table at the various executive vice presidents who headed up our major business units and simply said, "I don't want anyone coming back to me with attempts to reconcile or explain what we have heard today. What I want to happen is for us to change our performance in this area."

From that point forward, Mobil began giving a renewed priority to the company's environmental, health, and safety performance in its operations which spanned across 100-plus countries around the world. We began reporting on our environmental and safety performance on a quarterly basis just like we did with our financial performance. We set targets for that performance. We established an Environmental, Health, and Safety Management System that detailed specific requirements for every job having an impact on environment and safety, from a pipe fitter in a refinery to the chairman of the board. Every kind of operation was covered—drilling and production platforms for crude oil, natural gas plants, pipelines, refineries, terminals, warehouses, service stations, even administrative offices. We made environmental, safety, and health a significant factor in the appraisal of performance of every manager and executive, affecting his or her direct compensation. When I retired from Mobil three-and-a-half years later, Mobil had moved from seventh to second place in employee safety performance among the major international oil companies.

God does care about how we do our jobs and carry out our responsibilities. Lost time accidents are very costly, both to the employee and the company. Reducing accidents avoids injuries and saves lives, along with the associated costs amounting to potentially billions of dollars. An extreme but still real example is the 2010 explosion and oil spill from a BP drilling operation in the Gulf of Mexico, which resulted in eleven deaths, seventeen injuries, and an estimated cost to BP of as much as $40 billion in claims, litigation, and government actions.[1]

I felt like my actions in this matter were in line with what God wanted me to do, and his Spirit and presence in me gave me the courage and wisdom to move forward. While the name of Jesus was never mentioned, truth and integrity were being brought to the company's business processes. The kingdom of God was being furthered in Mobil through the stewardship of its most important asset—its employees—by the adoption of processes that resulted in the reduction of accidents, the saving of lives, and the conservation of resources.

Leading Others to Be Their Best

In the book *Spiritual Leadership*, Henry and Richard Blackaby say that the primary goal of spiritual leadership is taking people from where they are to where God wants them to be.[2] This should be an objective of every Christian having any supervisory responsibility for others in the workplace. Are a person's talents and abilities aligned with the duties and responsibilities of his or her job? Are they a good fit for what is expected of them?

Jim Savarese from Sacramento, California, has been involved in sales management for most of his career. At one point in the course of evaluating his staff, it became apparent that one of the sales representatives was not being as productive as he should be. While he was knowledgeable about the product and was good with detail in his communications, he was missing his quota on a regular basis, and his income was below the average for most other sales representatives. Jim concluded, "It was clear I needed to sit down with him and get to know him and his job history."

"His demeanor did not reveal the confidence necessary for him to be in the sales work he was doing," Jim said. "I asked him when he was happiest. He said it was when he was in the Marines and was responsible for implementing rules and regulations on a daily basis. As he spoke, it was clear he was enjoying just telling me about it. Even his body language changed. At the beginning of our discussion he was tense and defensive. As we continued he became calm and peaceful.

"I suggested that he consider changing positions from sales to a customer service representative job that required working constantly with details. He acknowledged that he was never comfortable in a quota environment. Within a few days Bob was transferred to customer service. To this day he is blossoming in a position that is adding greater value to both himself and the company.

Jim concludes, "I have often witnessed people in business who unfortunately find themselves working in drudgery because their work does not allow them to use their natural talents and gifts. For whatever reason—money, power, or necessity—they may be in a position that they aren't really suited for. I believe the Lord has gifted each of us with the potential to bloom in the workplace if we are using the gifts and talents given to us by God."

In this story we see Jim in his role as sales manager helping Bob discover his natural gifts and talents and leading him to a position that more fully suited those gifts. In doing so, Jim was serving not only his employer; he was also cooperating with the Holy Spirit in leading Bob to where God wanted him to be.

Relating to Colleagues, Subordinates, and Bosses

Nothing manifests the presence of Christ in you more than how you relate to others in the workplace, be they colleagues, subordinates, bosses, customers, or suppliers. In John 15:12 we read, "My command is this: Love each other as I have loved you. Greater love has no one than this, that he lay down his life for his friends." While you may have heard this Scripture many times, you may tend not to think of it applying to your employees, colleagues, or bosses. But Jesus was the master (boss) of his disciples. He was willing to (and in fact did) lay down his life for them and all humankind. Earlier in the Gospel of John, Jesus places this idea in the context of the workplace and characterizes himself as the good shepherd who lays down his life for his sheep. He contrasts himself with the hired hand who abandons the sheep when the wolf comes because the hired hand doesn't care about the sheep.

In the military we award the Congressional Medal of Honor to someone who has laid down his or her life, or at least put one's life at great risk for one's fellow soldiers. In the workplace, the circumstances are different, but there are still numerous opportunities to serve, to put others before yourself, to listen, encourage, teach, mentor, and sacrifice, as the stories that follow will illustrate.

Sacrificing Profits for Employees' Welfare

For many years, Jan Bento operated a fire prevention sprinkler business out of San Jose, California. One December, Jan received a request to install a sprinkler system for a large brokerage firm that was moving into a new building. One of the requirements was that the job had to be done immediately, and that meant that Jan's employees would have to work seven days a week over the Christmas holiday season.

Jan consulted with his design and construction managers, and they decided that it just wasn't right to expect their employees to work seven days a week, particularly over the Christmas season. "We have a good staff of employees who all have families to care for," said Jan. "While the phrase '24/7' originated here in Silicon Valley, we have not felt compelled to be drawn into its snare. In fact, when we bid jobs, we tell prospective customers that work on Sundays is not an option."

As a result, Jan responded to the prospective customer that his company would be happy to do the job if the time for completion could be extended. The customer declined, and Jan's firm did not get the business.

Jan, of course, would have made more money had he insisted that his employees take on this work, but he chose to consider the sacrifice it would have required of them and their families over the Christmas holidays. He put his employees before himself. I believe this is the kind of love Jesus was talking about.

Going the Extra Mile

Sometimes we serve or lay down our life for people in the workplace simply by taking the time to listen to their needs or concerns.

Diane McGinty from Gilroy, California, provides financial and insurance counseling to clients. One day, a client named Don came to her to seek advice about his 401K. He confided in her about his financial struggles since being laid off after many years working on the loading dock for a large manufacturing company. After a year of unemployment, he had finally gotten new work but was concerned about whether he would hurt his back by the heavy lifting required in the new job. He was fifty-nine years old.

Diane responded by telling Don that God wants to be with us in our struggles, and then she asked if she could pray with him. He consented, and Diane prayed that God would give him guidance and find just the right job, one that did not require heavy lifting.

Diane mentioned that there was a security guard company next door that might have some openings. She asked Don if he would like her to introduce him to them. He agreed, and it turned out that they had some open jobs. To apply for the job, however, Don had to download some forms from their website. He told Diane he wasn't sure he knew how to do that. Although her office was now closed, Diane brought him back and showed him how to download the material. She also called an employment counselor to set him up with an appointment to help him with his ongoing job search.

It was now after 6:30 p.m. Don said, "You know, I have really found that Christians are nice people." Diane asked, "Are you a Christian?" He said he was but that he didn't go to church. Diane then shared about her Christian faith and told Don about a ministry to which she belonged. She encouraged him and his wife to consider a weekend retreat the ministry was conducting.

In reflecting back on the experience, Diane observed, "When you hear someone say, 'I am having a hard time,' that is a signal from the Holy Spirit that we have an opening to bring the presence of Christ to that person. We build God's kingdom at work when we listen to someone's needs and act on them. It would have been so easy for me to go home and cook dinner after I answered his questions about his 401K. It was the end of the day, but I knew when he started to share his struggles that God wanted me to listen. Everyone we come in contact with should be touched by the grace of God." Diane concludes, "It is such a joyful life to be looking for opportunities to serve people God puts in my life so that they may receive the joy of Jesus. I have fun every day."

It is interesting to note that Diane was not initially trying to evangelize Don. Her first response was simply to listen to the concerns about his unemployment. Her second response was to act on those concerns by introducing him to the security guard company and assisting him in downloading and completing an application. Only when those needs were met, and after Don made the observation about Christians, did Diane share about her Christian faith. This is consistent with the instructions Jesus gave when he sent out the seventy two described in Chapter 10 of Luke's Gospel. Among his instructions were:

- When entering a house, extend your peace and stay in that house and receive whatever hospitality is offered. Do not move around from house to house.

- Heal the sick.

- Tell them, "The kingdom of God is near you."

Jesus was instructing his disciples that when they went out to meet people, they should stay put and build a relationship with them. After building a relationship and meeting their needs, then they could proclaim that the kingdom of God is at hand.

This same guide is applicable to Christians in the workplace. Get to know the people you work with. Focus on them. Listen to them. Seek to meet their needs where appropriate and possible. Love them. Then, if God opens the door, you can share your faith. You are being Christ and bringing his presence to others as much in the listening, coming to know them, and serving them as when you talk about Jesus and your faith.

Willingness to Work Together

In another story involving Jack McCall, the office manager for his insurance brokerage firm was diagnosed with cancer of the tongue and required surgery. She could no longer speak clearly, which was the most important part of her job. She asked Jack if she was going to be terminated for her inability to talk with the firm's customers. She was a little over a year from retirement, and losing her job at this point would have resulted in significant personal hardship. Jack decided to ask the firm's customers. He took the time to personally call over eighty customers to let them know of her condition and ask if they could work with her under the circumstances. He also asked for their prayers, understanding, and help. Jack said, "I knew they loved and respected Ginny, but I didn't know how much until their cards, letters, flowers, and gifts came pouring into our office." Both the employees in Jack's insurance company and the customers expressed the desire to work with her in spite of her disability, and she was able to work to her retirement age of sixty-five.

Here we see the kind of love Jesus was talking about. Jack took the time to call all of the firm's eighty customers to solicit their understanding and cooperation. We see love from the customers and the other employees in Jack's office in their willingness to work with Ginny in spite of her new disability.

Years later Ginny called to ask Jack if he would be with her when she was dying of cirrhosis of the liver. Jack observed, "What greater gift could one person give than to allow someone outside their family to be with them at the end? The choice to keep Ginny came out of prayer and God's love for her. The old Jack would have terminated her and most folks would have accepted that thinking. If I had, I really would have missed a gift from Ginny and some incredible blessing from God."

Love through Sacrifice

Sometimes being misunderstood by a boss, customer, or colleague can lead to harsh judgments about the kind of job we are doing. These misunderstandings can often lead to a loss of standing or even a job itself. How we react to these judgments says a lot about our Christian character. Steve Becker, a senior vice president with a major advertising firm in Minneapolis, chose not to contest a misunderstanding about his work because of the potentially negative impact on many of the employees who worked for him. This all culminated in Steve having lunch with the president of his agency and the CEO of the agency's largest client.

As Steve related, "I had never experienced a lunch like this. It appeared as if I were the main course. My first thought was that I was watching my career go down the tube, but at the same time I knew that God was in this moment and I was going to be fine."

The client's new CEO wanted Steve off the account. He was asking for Steve's head in front of his superiors. From the client's perspective, he thought he had justifiable reasons, although they were based upon inaccurate information. A misunderstanding had occurred and he was taking full advantage of the opportunity to establish his own advertising team. He turned the misunderstanding into a personal attack on Steve's character.

Steve's superiors were not going to jeopardize this large piece of business by defending him, and Steve wasn't asking them to do so. Forty people's livelihoods depended upon this client's business, and Steve was not going to put their jobs at risk by challenging the client's CEO. Steve's reputation was expendable for the sake of saving their jobs. He would face humiliation and misunderstanding from his peers and coworkers, but it was clear to Steve that this was his cross to carry.

Several weeks into the ordeal, an account supervisor who worked for Steve came into his office and said, "I just want you to know that I have never seen anyone go through a trial like this and handle it as you are doing. While I can't imagine what you are experiencing, I know it has to be your faith in God that is enabling you to do this." Hearing these words meant a great deal to Steve, because he had great respect for her. He had seen her progress from a career-driven "yuppie" to a person who was a real asset to the business, as well as a fine mother of a young boy and someone who was actively involved in her church.

Two years later, Steve was laid off from the agency during a downturn in business. He went on to work briefly for another agency and then started his own consulting business. Today he heads the marketing operations of a transportation company. Steve concludes, "As difficult as this was, in many ways it was a time of grace. It was a combination of knowing that I was doing exactly what God wanted and a clear sense of God's presence."

Steve accepted God's will that he put forty other employees before the security of his own position and trusted that God would have other work for him. "Greater love has no one than this, that he lay down his life [position] for his friends" (Jn 15:13).

Loving the Boss

In considering the relationship between a boss and employee, we tend to think about the boss's responsibility for looking out for the interests of the employee, but not necessarily the employee looking out for the interests of the boss. Several years ago during my morning prayer time, I found myself praying for my boss, who headed up the legal operations for Mobil's US Marketing and Refining operations. He was an exacting boss, but he was a good person with great integrity. While praying, I received the thought, "Why are you limiting your prayers just for your direct boss—why not also his boss and the entire management team, up to and including your CEO and board of directors? Pray for wisdom, integrity, and love in how they oversee the operations of the company. Your prayers can impact areas and operations of the company far beyond your immediate responsibilities and sphere of influence."

This was a new revelation to me. As Christians in the workplace, through prayer we have the opportunity to impact more than just the confines of our particular job or position. We can intercede for the Father's grace to impact even our bosses and the decisions they make. We may or may not see the direct results of our prayer, but we should never underestimate the power and influence they bring to the workplace.

Encouraging the CEO

Will DeSanto worked for a large power company in Minneapolis that had been receiving some unfavorable press due to the actions of one of its subsidiaries. The subsidiary had incurred significant debt, which had an adverse impact on revenues, earnings, and the stock price of the company. As a result, the senior management of the parent company was under a lot of pressure from the media, shareholders, employees, and customers.

One day on his way to work, the thought came to Will that he should do something to encourage the CEO of the company. At first Will dismissed the idea because he was nervous about approaching the CEO, whom he did not know or have any contact with in his normal work activities as a property services engineer. In fact, their offices were in separate buildings. Still, the idea kept coming back that he should do something. As Will was approaching the office complex, he noticed a parking spot on the street right outside the executive office building. Will parked and proceeded into the building, all the while figuring that it was not likely that he would have the opportunity to see or say anything to the CEO.

As Will walked toward the elevator, he encountered the CEO along with one of the vice presidents. Will took this as a sign that he should act on his idea. As they walked into the elevator together, Will introduced himself to the CEO and told him he thought he was doing an excellent job in the face of much adverse publicity. He encouraged him to persevere, and then told the CEO that he was praying for him. The CEO thanked him, and then, as he was getting off the elevator, he said to Will, "You will never know how much your words and prayers mean to me."

Will was astonished. "I would have never dreamed that I would ever have the chance to personally encourage the head of our company," Will said. "The Holy Spirit provided me with the idea, the opportunity, and the courage. I just acted on what was happening in front of me."

God's love knows no boundaries, nor is it limited by class, title, or position. It only needs someone to give it expression. That's what Will was doing—allowing God's love, encouragement, and support for the CEO to be expressed through him.

Encouragement, Healing, and New Life in Christ

Another story involving encouragement and prayers comes from Steve Harless, a superintendent for a commercial construction firm in Sacramento, California. He not only encouraged his boss, he also brought healing and Christian baptism to the boss' family.

"Several years ago I began a project with a new project manager who was recovering from surgery for the removal of a large cancerous tumor at the base of his spine. While he had the reputation of being very demanding and sometimes difficult to work with, he was very open about the surgery, indicating that it gave him a new outlook on life. We talked briefly about God and church.

He was aware of my involvement in Christians in Commerce, and occasionally, when no one else was around, he would start a conversation about his church or my faith, but he wouldn't allow it to go very far and would soon change the subject. I started to pray for him, and I asked the men in Christians in Commerce to pray that God would help me to recognize the opportunity to do his will and the courage to follow it.

"About six months into the project, he learned that the tumor had returned and was even larger than the first tumor. He informed the project team that he was going to have surgery again and that it was going to be even more radical than before. I wanted to do something for him but didn't know what to do. I began praying for God to show me, and he did.

"I drafted a letter about the real effects of the power of prayer for people undergoing surgery. I cited a newspaper article in which doctors had confirmed the beneficial effects they had observed from the power of prayer on patients, something that would appeal to the analytical nature of this manager. I then circulated it throughout the company and asked people to commit to spending time praying for him on the day of his surgery. I suggested that even though we couldn't be with him in the hospital, we could be with him in spirit. In spite of the short notice, signatures were quickly added to the letter indicating people's commitment to pray. I placed the letter in an envelope and put it in his truck on his last day.

"The next morning, a Saturday, he called me at home, something he had never done. After discussing some project-related issues, there was a brief pause and then he said that the letter really meant a lot to him. As I hung up the phone, my wife said, 'I think you were put on this project by God for this manager.'

"His surgery was a success. About two months later he came to the project site to review progress with the team. After everyone had left, he came over to my desk and told me that he had some good news to share. He said, 'I knew you would be happy to hear that I got baptized this weekend. In fact, my whole family was baptized.'"

Steve was indeed very happy about the success of the surgery and his boss and family being baptized. He was also blessed to see that the prayers he had initiated with his colleagues on behalf of his boss had been answered. By reaching out to his boss, writing a letter of encouragement, seeking signatures from his colleagues, and being regularly available to talk with his boss about his surgery and matters of God, Steve put his love, faith, and courage into action. As the Apostle John says, "Let us not love with words or tongue, but with actions" (1 Jn 3:18).

Questions for Reflection and Discussion

1. How have you experienced the Holy Spirit influencing your actions in the workplace relative to integrity in your daily choices and business decisions? Are you tempted to tell your boss what he wants to hear or the truth on a given problem? Are you forthcoming with your employees and customers?

2. How have you sought to be a good steward of your talents,

time, possessions and responsibilities? Are you seeking God's will in each of these areas?

3. How has God worked through you in your relationships with colleagues, the development of your subordinates and supporting your boss? Do you enable your employees to be their best? Do you treat colleagues and customers with respect?

4. How do you reflect Christ in your workplace? Can you do so without mentioning his name? Describe how.

Chapter Five

TRANSFORMING
THE WORK ENVIRONMENT

Workplace environments have a huge effect on employee productivity, morale, and well-being. The following stories illustrate how both the boss and the employee can impact the workplace environment when they let the presence of God in them affect how they relate to one another.

A Dentist with a Difference

Dr. Bill Nanna has had a dental practice in Sterling, Virginia, for over thirty years. One day he noticed that one of the hygienists was showing signs of depression. "It was clear that she was very down, and her life did not appear to have much joy or happiness," Bill said. "I talked with her and tried to find out what was going on. She indicated that she could hardly get out of bed in the morning. She said that no matter what she did, nothing seemed to work in terms of lifting the heaviness from her life. That's when I mentioned that she might think about looking into joining a church. Her response was, 'I am about as religious as a fence post.' I told her that I would pray for her.

"The rest of my staff and I had been previously talking about starting some type of Bible study in the office. We were all concerned about Carol. One of the staff suggested that we start the Bible study and then invite Carol. Not only did Carol accept our invitation, she rearranged her schedule to be in the office every Tuesday when we met over the lunch hour. At one of our meetings she said, 'I used to think that things in life were controlled by fate, but now I see that we can ask Jesus to be in control.'"

Bill observes, "Our small group Tuesday meetings are not only impacting Carol, they are also affecting the entire staff in how they are treating each other and dealing with patients. Often our patients share certain needs or problems. We respond with an offer to pray for them, sometimes on the spot."

After performing a root canal on one of his patients on a Friday, Bill received a call from the patient's wife on Sunday to report that her husband was doing very poorly. From all that she described, Bill thought it was something more serious than a possible infection from the root canal, and he suggested that she take him to the emergency room. After a couple days of tests, the husband was diagnosed with acute lymphatic leukemia. Bill informed his six-person office staff, and they started praying for the husband, both collectively and individually.

"The husband underwent treatment for several months and we continued to pray for him," Bill said. "We arranged for a local pastor to call on him to offer prayer and support. The patient's wife was very appreciative and would stop by the office to give us updates and bring us flowers from her garden. The patient's leukemia went into remission, and his wife asserts that it was a miracle which she attributes to our prayers.

"Months later she called to say that her husband came down with the H1N1 flu virus, and because of his weakened immune system, he went into a coma. We immediately began praying for him once again. Several people in the office prepared meals to take to the couple. The husband was barely responsive for two weeks. Fortunately, he survived and seems to be recovering. His wife is calling it 'another miracle.' She said, 'Without your prayers he would have never survived.'

"What stuck out to me," Bill said, "was that as soon as her husband came down with the H1N1 flu, she called us, a dental office, to ask for prayer." Bill allowed the presence of God in him to be manifested to his office staff and patients. The result was a staff motivated to serve each other and Bill's patients, and all are the better for it.

Christ's YMCA

For many years Kirby Falkenberg was the CEO of the YMCA Michiana, headquartered in South Bend, Indiana. Early on, Kirby approached his work and responsibility as a vocation that furthered God's kingdom right in the middle of his work circumstances. When Kirby first heard he was being considered for the CEO position, he wasn't sure he wanted it because the board had a reputation for firing its CEOs. Nevertheless, Kirby had the reputation of turning around problem YMCAs, and the board began to actively pursue him.

Although the new position was a career advancement for Kirby, that was not his first priority. "My number one priority was to determine whether the board would support me in carrying out the true mission of the YMCA, including its Christian heritage," said Kirby. "Since I wasn't seeking the job, I was able to be bold with the board's search committee in asking some tough questions. I asked, 'Do you think Christ has any impact here? How would I know it is Christ's Y?' There was a long silence, and then I said, 'The only way I would take this job is if the South Bend YMCA is truly a Christian organization.' We then discussed who owned the Y—the board or its members? While some of them thought the board owned the Y, I explained that the organization needed to be member-focused, just like a business needs to be customer-focused."

Kirby was offered the job. His first action was a meeting with all 200 employees to review his expectations for them, including how the organization and all of its branches should operate with integrity and high moral conduct. Kirby said, "As I began to review job descriptions, I noticed that the purpose of most jobs was expressed in how much money a particular function could produce rather than how it was to serve members. So I spent time with each department head, reviewing the vision and mission of the Y and how their particular department was to serve the members. We moved from a dollar-driven Y to a mission-driven Y, with the primary emphasis on better serving our members. Our goal is to welcome every member and help them connect with a particular group so everyone feels included.

"We try to set a very positive tone. For example, some of the handball players had a tendency to use rather rough and crude language. It could be heard by anyone who happened to be in that part of the Y. I said, 'Look fellas, you have to clean up your language because it is setting a bad tone and making others uncomfortable.' These expletives are no longer used around our YMCA.

"All of this has had an impact on our operations. Membership has doubled. We have gone from a $900,000 cumulative deficit to an operating surplus. We have raised $2,600,000 for capital improvements to upgrade our facilities, all of which is better serving our customers."

Kirby has been advancing God's kingdom by changing the environment and culture of the organization he heads. While it is a Christian organization which enables Kirby the freedom to talk about whether it is "Christ's Y," his actions in changing the environment could be applied to most business organizations as well.

Prayer in the Workplace

If there are other Christians where you work, it might be possible to join with them to pray for your workplace environment, the employer for whom you work, or the needs of other employees. This kind of prayer, of course, must not interfere with your first responsibility to do the work that is expected of you. The following story, although taking place in the context of a Christian publisher, nevertheless illustrates the blessing that can accrue to the participants, the employer, and the people for whom prayer may be directed.

Just Do It

Jennifer Ellis is part of a nine-person staff of a bimonthly newspaper for a Christian organization with over 100 employees. "The main reason I took this job was to have my faith and my work more interconnected," said Jennifer. "When I started a couple of years ago, I had some preconceived idea about what it would be like in a Christian workplace. What I found was that, even when people share a common faith and have opportunities to pray together, they often don't.

"For nearly two years, one of my coworkers and I talked about praying together, but we could never figure out how to make it work due to schedule conflicts, management changes, etc. We both felt that something was missing from our work and that neither of us was truly living out our faith in our workplace. After growing in our friendships with other coworkers and understanding that many of us were experiencing the same hunger for Christ, the idea of group prayer again surfaced.

"We had a group of five people willing to start meeting for prayer [before work]. At first we struggled with issues on format, how to be inclusive of others, and what to include in our meetings. Finally, I said, 'Let's just start meeting, and we'll tweak things as we go.'

"We have now been meeting for about three months. Sometimes events or the press of work will get in the way, but we have kept going. Not only does our prayer time bless our day, but sharing intentions and needs for prayer has developed a sense of community among us. It has created a greater interest in each other and a greater level of care for one another. It has also allowed us to encourage and help each other through our challenges.

"It also provides an opportunity to resolve conflicts. Recently, I volunteered for an assignment that had the effect of excluding a coworker from doing the work, and she was offended. If we had not been praying together, I would have never been able to pick up on what was happening, talk it out honestly with her, and reconcile with her.

"There have been other blessings. My twenty-one-year old cousin was diagnosed with non-Hodgkin's lymphoma. We started to pray for her on a continuing basis. Today, she has fully recovered and is returning to school.

"In another blessing, one of our staff writers desired the opportunity to participate in more mission-oriented journalism. We prayed for her, and she has since been awarded a scholarship to participate in a program covering mission work in South America, one of only twenty from around the world and the only person selected from the United States."

What advice does Jennifer offer to people who are thinking about gathering for regular prayer in their office? "Just do it. Be with God, even if there are only two of you. Others will follow. Working for a Christian organization may be more tolerant of people coming together in prayer, but many of the same obstacles you find in any other workplace are still present. While I find that I need to be sensitive to other people in the office, I also need to be bold and courageous. Other employees have witnessed us in prayer and it is inspiring them to incorporate more prayer into their lives. I am much more peaceful on the days we pray together."

Prayer on the Battlefield

Here is another story about fellow workers praying together, not in an office or factory, but on a battlefield. Tom Kelly, who retired in 2010 as a colonel in the Marine Corps Reserve, had multiple tours in Afghanistan and Iraq. He served as director of Counter-Improvised Explosive Devices and as a senior Marine for the US Marine Forces Central Command.

"During my tours in Iraq and Afghanistan, I've had the privilege of observing young military men and women from all services. Most were on their third or fourth tours, and I was amazed at the remarkable courage, commitment, and self-sacrifice that they displayed. They have been successful in gaining the support of the indigenous population by overcoming fear and demonstrating a genuine concern for the welfare of others.

"As a senior officer, my responsibility was to travel to each unit in the field and ensure they had the resources needed. Afghanistan, in particular, is a very austere environment, and most of the infantry Marines I visited were continuously in harm's way as they worked with the local population and patrolled remote areas where Taliban insurgents set up explosives and ambushes. Most units were replenished by helicopter once a week. Some units did not have access to a chaplain or religious services for several weeks. I often marveled at how squads of young Marines between the ages of nineteen and twenty-four, led by a corporal, would endure the same stress and dangers each day.

"A common practice I observed before a squad would go on patrol was to form a prayer circle. The men would gather together, putting their hands on each other's shoulders. They would collectively ask the Lord for his protection and guidance. They would pray for the wounded or deceased, for a family issue back home, and they would recite Psalm 23:4, which some refer to as the 'Soldier's Prayer': 'Even though I walk through the valley of the shadow of death, I will fear no evil, for you are with me; your rod and your staff, they comfort me.'

"These prayer circles are not part of any military training but were initiated informally at the small unit level. In most cases, a member of the squad, not the squad leader, initiates the prayer circle. What I noted as the troops mounted their vehicles following the prayer was that they seemed at peace, joyful, and confident. In many ways, this peace and self-control resonated throughout their patrol engagements with local Afghans and helped the Marines foster a strong relationship with the Afghan people they were protecting. The close bond formed by the squad that prayed together helped them overcome nearly any adversity."

"Marines and other US military personnel would often

spend their free time volunteering to visit local orphanages or camps filled with thousands of refugees recently returning after being forced to flee to Pakistan during the decades of occupation by the Soviets, Mujahedeen, or Taliban. The charity, humanitarian assistance, and kindness resulting from these efforts have had a profound influence on Afghan citizens. Despite the threats of traversing mountainous trails often saturated with mines and explosive devices, Marines would never avoid engaging with the Afghan or Iraqi people. They knew that their generosity, candor, and daily assistance were making a difference in cultivating trust and gaining public support."

Employees Supporting One Another

Justin Bratnober owns Trademark Transportation, a freight-forwarding business that specializes in the transportation of refrigerated products throughout the country, with warehouses in Minneapolis and Chicago. Justin says, "Our first priority is to understand our customers and to serve their needs. I make it a point to meet at least monthly with all of our employees, including those on the loading docks. We ask them to share stories about how we can better serve our customers and work as a team to do so.

"At one of these meetings, a Chicago warehouse employee shared the following story. Late one Friday night, a truck carrying products arrived from a customer in Indianapolis to be delivered to its customers in both Chicago and Minneapolis. The truck had been loaded in a very random way with individual orders mixed up and paperwork not matching the orders. The employee, who had already put in a full day, could have just offloaded the items to be delivered in Chicago and sent the truck on its way to Minneapolis. He wasn't expected to do anything more.

"Instead, he said, 'Why don't we unload the whole truck and reload it correctly for the guys in Minneapolis?' It took two employees four hours, working into the wee hours of Saturday morning, to identify, sort, and reload a multitude of orders and products destined for Minneapolis. This is a small story that could go unnoticed, but it is really huge because it reflects an attitude of the employees in Chicago who wanted to support the employees in Minneapolis who had just gone through a difficult time of changing warehouse locations."

Justin observes, "When I started this business, my personal financial security was my first priority. The Lord changed my heart several years ago, and now my desire is to serve and glorify the Lord in the work that I do and our company does. This desire and constant prayer has had a huge impact on me and how we operate our company."

In another example, Justin reports, "One summer we discovered that we were going to have too many managers gone at the same time in Minneapolis where people tend to covet their summer vacations. An employee from Chicago agreed to come to Minneapolis to help out, and other employees in both locations agreed to redistribute some of the work in order to provide the needed coverage. Again, we had employees with a willingness to support each other to support the overall mission of our company.

"A consultant once told me," Justin concludes, "that the best brand promise is not one that is expressed but one that is felt or experienced. I think the same is true in how we serve the Lord in our work. What counts is how I live it out, like our staff has demonstrated. My job is to serve the Lord by providing a place where people have the opportunity to participate in his work in

the marketplace and leading our employees to work coopera-
tively in understanding the real needs of our customers and in
meeting those needs."

Justin has created a work environment that clearly sets out
the mission of the company and encourages the employees to
work as a team to serve customers and one another in fulfilling
the mission. The motivation for Justin is his love of God and his
desire to serve God by building his kingdom in the marketplace.
The kingdom is being built by Justin seeking excellence in the
transportation of refrigerated products and in providing a work
environment that fosters respect for employees and serves the
needs of customers.

Opportunities for Forgiveness

When it comes to the workplace, our first reaction may be
that forgiveness is rare and not even to be expected, but Jesus'
call to forgiveness was not limited in the scope, context, or type
of relationship to which it applied. The workplace offers many
opportunities for offense, hurt, and injustice. If we are to be
Christ and bring his presence to the workplace, we need to be
open to offering apology and seeking forgiveness where we have
offended someone, or similarly, being willing to forgive when we
have been offended.

We are familiar with the words in the Lord's Prayer where
Jesus says that we should ask the Father to "forgive us our debts,
as we also have forgiven our debtors" (Mt 6:12). This is the only
verse in the Lord's Prayer that Jesus goes on to explain, illustrat-
ing the importance he placed on it. He says, "For if you forgive
men when they sin against you, your heavenly Father will also
forgive you. But if you do not forgive men their sins, your Father

will not forgive your sins" (Mt 6:14-15). This is a pretty tough statement. If we don't forgive others, we can't expect God to forgive us. The irony is that it is not so much our offenders who are hurt by our lack of forgiveness, but us. We hurt ourselves by holding on to hurts, slights, or other offenses from others. Unforgiveness results in anger, resentment, jealousy, agitation, broken relationships, and disunity in a work environment just as much as it does in a marriage, family, or friendship. The fruit of forgiveness is reconciliation, strengthened relationships, greater cooperation, and unity—all important to the efficient operation of any business or work environment.

Bill Blauvelt of South Bend, Indiana, taught high-school business classes for fifteen years. He then earned a master's degree that qualified him to begin work in counseling. He initiated an application for a $250,000 grant for his school district, which enabled the district to hire four people in vocational counseling.

"Through the grant I was able to work with the students while administering the grant—a position I very much enjoyed," said Bill. "A year into the program, there was a change of administration and I had a new boss. I subsequently found myself back in the kind of teaching job that I had previously. My boss told me there was an emergency vacancy in another school, and because of a hiring freeze I had to take the job. It was clear to me, however, that my new boss wanted his own person in the position I was holding.

"Needless to say, I was angry. I felt the change was unjust, and I found myself blaming my boss. Many told me that I should have been given his position when the change in administration took place. For nearly six months I was very preoccupied with anger and resentment. It affected my attitude and performance.

At the time I wasn't really looking for advancement, but my ego got a hold of me. 'You're better than that,' I told myself. 'You're not being treated fairly.'

"Then one day at a meeting of the South Bend chapter of Christians in Commerce, I heard a teaching on forgiveness that said, 'As a result of forgiveness, everyone is set free. The wrongdoer is released from obligation, guilt, and shame. The victim is released from indignation, anger, and bitterness. And the Lord releases more of himself.'

"This really hit me; it was a turning point for me. I prayed for the strength to forgive and to let go of my anger, and my prayers were answered. I was able to forgive my boss and the injustice that was done to me. Almost immediately, I had a new outlook and peace of mind. The Lord gave me the grace to forgive and truly let go of my anger and frustration. My life was changed, perhaps only in a small way, but definitely in a way that meant a great deal to me.

"A year later I went back into counseling in the same area that I had been previously. I kept the same boss for the next fifteen years, and we enjoyed a relationship of mutual respect."

Bill concludes, "I thank God for blessing me with a wonderful career of teaching high-school and middle-school students for many years. I also thank him for freeing me from a time of anger and resentment that could have distracted me from the calling he had for me."

Setting the Prisoners Free

Let's look at another story about forgiveness, as well as compassion and obedience, involving Bob Schumacher, whose story on integrity appeared earlier. Bob had invested several thousand dollars in a new company that was to provide specialized insurance products and services. Initially, the new company did well, and Bob's investment multiplied nine-fold. Then Bob and other investors came to realize that one of the partners, Steve, was not conducting operations in a totally ethical way. Bob and the other investors withdrew their support from the company, which resulted in its going out of business. Bob lost all of his investment. He was naturally angry with Steve and what he had done. Sometime later Bob learned that Steve had been convicted of embezzlement in another business venture and had been sent to prison.

"After reading about this in the newspaper," Bob said, "I began to sense that the Lord wanted me to go visit Steve in prison. My first reaction was 'No way!' I was still angry with him for what he had done. Still, I was prompted to go.

"When I walked into the visitor's area, Steve was shocked to see me. It had been seven years. Tears started to well up in his eyes. He couldn't believe that someone whom he had previously hurt would come to visit him. He was a different man. In contrast to the glib and confident manner that I remembered, he was very humble. He acknowledged that he needed to change. He had been attending a Bible study in prison and was open to talk about spiritual matters. I felt such compassion for him. I prayed with him and suggested that, while he was going through a very painful time, it could also be a time of God's grace. I encouraged him to be open to that grace. I visited him a couple more times and each time we would read Scripture and pray.

"When Steve was released from prison, I bought him a Bible and took him to lunch. 'Here is the instruction manual for our lives,' I said. He was very receptive. He observed, 'In AA, people have sponsors and regular meetings. What is there for a new Christian?' I invited him to join a group of Christian business-men with whom I regularly met. At one point during the lunch, my cell phone rang. I told Steve that ordinarily I would never answer a phone while with someone else, but I had a client that had a significant need. He said, 'You don't know how blessed you are to have a client with a need that you can serve.' I found myself being encouraged and blessed by Steve while I was trying to bless and encourage him. I asked if he needed any financial assistance. He patted the Bible and said, 'You have already given me the assistance that I need.'"

Bob concludes, "I don't know where this will all lead. I believe this renewed connection with Steve is about God dealing with my unforgiving heart as much as it is about Steve's spiritual journey. I know my heart has been changed. It appears that Steve has been touched by the Lord. Now he is blessing me."

Nothing interferes more with our relationship with God than unforgiveness. Anger, bitterness, and resentment rob us of our peace and serve as a wedge, not only with the person with whom we are angry but also with God. Jesus said, "Therefore, if you are offering your gift at the altar and there remember that your brother has something against you, leave your gift there in front of the altar. First go and be reconciled to your brother; then come offer your gift" (Mt 5:23-24). Jesus is telling us that reconciliation should take place before we come to him in prayer and worship. Otherwise, the lack of reconciliation will serve as an obstacle in our coming to know him, understanding his word, and taking on his mind. He affirms the better way in the Beati-tudes when he says, "Blessed are the peacemakers, for they will be called sons of God" (Mt 5:9).

Physical Healing in the Workplace

Like forgiveness, you may think that prayers for healing are not appropriate or normal for the workplace. Yet the workplace is full of people who have needs, including illnesses and infirmities. Obviously, filling these needs is not the primary purpose of most workplaces, unless perhaps you work in a medical care facility. The primary purpose of most workplaces is the delivery of goods and services. Nevertheless, in the course of your relationships, you may have an opportunity to bring Christ's healing presence to those with whom you work. For this to occur, there usually needs to be a relationship of trust that has been built over years of working together.

I remember praying for one of our executives at Mobil who was diagnosed with inoperable brain cancer. We had worked together at various times for over twenty years. I was in his office one day, and he shared his anguish and concerns for himself and his family. I offered to pray with him and he accepted. I prayed for healing and peace for him and his family. On another occasion, I was at lunch with another manager who had been one of my internal company's legal clients for several years. He shared about some difficulties he was experiencing in his marriage. I reached across the table, put my hand on his arm, and prayed for reconciliation. He and his wife were later reconciled.

I never tried to wear my Christianity on my sleeve, but over time people would come to my office on occasion to share various problems or needs. These included attorneys who reported to me, clerical staff, other managers, and colleagues. Most of the time I would offer to pray with them. I don't remember anyone ever refusing the offer. As I look back on these occasions, they were probably fewer than they should have been, given the fact that I was trying to seek the Lord and his will over the last twenty-two years of my career.

"The Tumor Is Gone!"

Generally, it takes opportunity, discernment, and faith to pray with a work colleague. Dr. Sheri Donaldson, a physical therapist who works at St. Joseph Outpatient Rehabilitation Center in Phoenix, Arizona, tells about her experience with a coworker, Ashley.

"Every two years, Ashley must go for an MRI and a follow-up visit with her neurosurgeon in connection with surgery she had a few years ago to remove a brain tumor. It is always a time of anxiety for her because there was a piece of the brain tumor that could not be reached and continues to be seen on the MRI. The last time she was due for an MRI, she told me how scared she was, wondering if the tumor would grow and come back. I told her I would pray for her, but I felt like I walked away from what I was supposed to do—pray *with* her.

"I told Ashley that I prayed with a small group of women each Wednesday morning, and I would ask them to pray for her because I had seen amazing things happen when they prayed. When the small group met, I mustered up the courage to ask that the little piece of tumor would be gone in the name of Jesus, and the group prayed in agreement.

"It just so happened that the following day I got to see Ashley right before she left for her appointment. I kept asking the Lord if he really wanted me to share our prayer with her and literally put my hand on her forehead. This was scary because I didn't want to hurt her by an incorrect word. Well, there she was, all by herself, telling me it was time and looking very nervous. I shared with her that we prayed that when the MRI came back, the tumor would be gone. Then I placed my hand on her forehead and blessed her. She gave me a hug and went out the door.

"The next time we saw each other, I was walking down the hallway past her office when she said, 'Sheri, the tumor is gone!' That's right, there was no trace of it on the MRI! Later, Ashley asked if I would take her to Mass with me. She started going to a church that is within walking distance of her house. Also, our relationship has developed in such a way that she is much more open to talk about faith issues.

"A couple of years passed, and Ashley had another meeting with her neurosurgeon to review the most recent MRI. He said the films looked 'awesome.' She came right over to me and gave me a big hug and shared the good news."

Sheri concludes, "This experience has also had an impact on me. I am much more alert to whether the Lord wants me to reach out to others and be available to talk with them and to pray with them if the need arises. Others have asked me to pray with them. One coworker asked me to pray for her with respect to some forgiveness issues in her life and a diagnosis of cancer. Another asked me to pray with her for the needs of some of her patients. She has even been called from other parts of the hospital for me to pray with her over the phone. I just keep asking the Holy Spirit for the grace to hear him."

We see in Sheri's story someone who is not pushing her Christianity on others in her workplace. In fact, her inclination was not to reach out, but her love for God and her friend, together with the power of the Holy Spirit, provided the opportunity and the courage for her to do so. In the course of all of this, she was able to maintain her professionalism and discretion.

An Extraordinary Miracle

This next story involves John DeSanto, the prosecutor from Duluth, Minnesota. This story may seem a bit out of the ordinary to some, but as far as John is concerned, he was just following the example of St. Paul as recorded in the Book of Acts.

In the course of John's work, he has a lot of contact with police officers. One of the officers, a detective sergeant named Eric, informed John that he had lymphatic cancer and was about to begin chemotherapy sessions. Eric was in his mid-thirties, married with two children. John said, "I immediately put my hand on the back of his neck and prayed for healing in the name of Jesus Christ. I put his name in my prayer log and prayed for him every day."

After a couple of months of chemotherapy, Eric lost his hair and was often too weak to come to work. About this time Eric testified in court on a murder case that John was prosecuting. John could see that Eric was very ill, so he asked Eric if he would attend an upcoming Christian conference in Minneapolis in order to be prayed with for healing. John explained that the healing power of Jesus had been manifested in the past at these conferences. Eric said he was open to going, but he had an additional chemotherapy scheduled and was too weak to make the trip. John told him he would pray for him there.

In Acts 19:11-12, Luke reports, "God did extraordinary miracles through Paul, so that even handkerchiefs and aprons that had touched him were taken to the sick, and their illnesses were cured." At the conference John stood in for Eric, as people gathered around him to pray that Eric's cancer would be healed. Someone handed John a handkerchief that was prayed over to take back to Eric.

After returning to Duluth, John met Eric one day in the courthouse and invited him into his office. John said, "I told him that we had prayed for his healing at the conference, and someone had given me a handkerchief, which we prayed over for him. I emphasized that I firmly believed in the healing power of Jesus Christ and that God could use the handkerchief as a sign of our faith just as had been done in biblical times to heal him. We placed the handkerchief on his chest and prayed that the healing power of Jesus Christ would remove the cancer from him. He thanked me and told me he believed that he would be healed and would return the handkerchief after the doctors had confirmed that he no longer had cancer." About a month later Eric informed John that the doctors had confirmed that he no longer had cancer. This took place in the fall of 2001. As of the writing of this book, ten years later, Eric is still cancer-free.

Sometimes our willingness to step out and do something that may seem to be foolish reflects the kind of faith on which God wishes to act, even in our workplaces.

Introducing Customers and Colleagues to Jesus

God's plan to bring his presence to the workplace by working through you is not about using the workplace to evangelize, although it can have that effect. When we are at work, our primary purpose is to further the mission of our employer. At the same time, in the course of contributing our part to this mission, we have the opportunity to reflect God in our conduct and character in contrast with the ways of the world. This sometimes opens the door to people wanting to know the reason behind our contrasting conduct. Why are we different? They may, in fact, be attracted to the Spirit of God that is in us as manifested by our conduct. It is at these times that we may have the opportunity to share who we are, why we act as we do, and introduce someone to Jesus and the presence of the Holy Spirit. As St. Peter said, "Always be prepared to give an answer to everyone who asks you to give the reason for the hope that you have" (1 Pt 3:15). In Mark Green's book, *Thank God It's Monday,* he says, "The workplace is, day in, day out, the one place where non-Christians can see the difference that being a Christian makes."[1]

The Fruit of His Labor

Ken Balestrieri has been in the business of distributing fruits and vegetables out of Salinas, California, to clients throughout the world for over thirty years. He has always been very open with clients and friends about his Catholic faith and in talking about the ministry of Christians in Commerce (CIC), inviting them to weekly meetings and weekend retreats.

Gordon, one of his clients from New York, was visiting to tour various crop areas. Ken reports, "We were in San Louis Obispo on a Thursday, which happened to coincide with the local Christians in Commerce breakfast meeting, so I asked Gordon if he would like to attend. Because he had heard me talk about CIC before, he had an interest, especially since there would be some local growers and agro-businessmen that he could meet. He asked what went on at the meetings, and I explained the format of worship, prayer, and fellowship.

Although he had been raised with a Buddhist background, his new wife was Presbyterian and his interest in Christianity was growing. I asked him if he had been baptized in the Holy Spirit. He said he was not familiar with the Holy Spirit, and I explained the Trinity and the role of the Father, Son and Holy Spirit in our lives.

Ken continues, "We went to the meeting, and it was a wonderful gathering of spirit-filled men. We sang and worshiped God, heard a challenging teaching, and experienced great fellowship. Before the close of the meeting, I asked the men if they would pray with Gordon. We laid hands on him and prayed for him to receive the power of the Holy Spirit.

"After he returned to New York, we had many conversations about the Lord and his many gifts to us. I asked him if he had a Bible. He said no, so I sent him one. He began to read and study it. We then began to have ongoing Scripture discussions. Gordon also began to attend the local Presbyterian church with his wife on a regular basis. After several years of experiencing difficulty conceiving a child, Gordon and his wife began praying for a child. Two years later his wife gave birth to a baby boy. They named him Matthew, 'a gift from God.' After Matthew's birth, he registered his family as members of the Presbyterian church. A few years later he was asked to become a deacon, and he joyfully accepted."

Ken established a long-standing relationship with Gordon in which there was respect on both a business and personal level. Because of the trust that was built up, the stage was set for Ken to talk about his Christian faith and invite Gordon to a Christian business fellowship. We also see Ken's concern for Gordon in the way that he followed up with him, bought him a Bible, and continued to encourage him to study Scripture and join a church. Fortunately, Ken was able to see the fruit of his labor with Gordon joining his wife's church, having his son baptized, and later becoming a deacon in that church.

His Life's Work Is Christ's Work

Jack McCall, the insurance broker from San Jose, California, tells about a vision he received in 1987. "I was walking down this incredibly beautiful beach," Jack said. "I was in awe that I was the only one there to enjoy it. As I continued to walk, I realized that I was not alone. At the far end, I noticed what looked like another man. I was too far away to know what he was doing. As I got closer to him, it appeared that he was motioning with his arm for me to come to him.

I continued toward him casually until I noticed that his call was urgent. Then I ran as fast as I could to reach him. He was pulling in this huge net that extended out into the ocean. I automatically reached down to help and noticed that instead of being filled with fish, the net was filled with human faces. I was stunned. I looked over at the man I had come to help, and I realized it was Jesus."

Jack continues, "This was before I surrendered my life to Jesus Christ. I didn't really know that Jesus had placed it on my heart to make my life's work his work. There is an urgency to help him now. Thoughts of resting or retiring to live out my last days have fallen by the wayside. I know now that I, too, had been just another face in the net. He used others to rescue me, and now he is asking me to die to my own desire and do likewise. How could I not?"

Dealing with Terminal Illness

There is an urgency in sharing the Good News with those who may be struggling with sin, illness, or disorder in their lives, with those who have not experienced Jesus Christ or invited him into their lives. Nowhere is this more critical than reaching out to a business colleague who is terminally ill.

A Grateful Family

Ruth Wehner of Sacramento, California, had a coworker, Stella, who was diagnosed with terminal cancer. As the illness progressed, Ruth frequently talked with Stella on the phone. "Very soon I came to realize that the Lord was putting it on my heart to bring his word to Stella," Ruth observed. "My first reaction was apathy and denial. 'Lord, are you sure you want me to do this? I'm not sure I know how. I'm not very good at this sort of thing.' Finally, after lots of prayer, several sleepless nights, and encouragement from other Christian friends, I asked if she was receiving visitors. She said yes and also mentioned that she had been having several dreams recently and that I was in each of them. I took this as a sign that the Holy Spirit was bringing us together.

"When I visited her the following day, she spoke of her religious upbringing as a child; she asked about the right way to pray and wondered whether her illness was the result of something bad she had done in her life. I assured her that that was not the case, and that God loved her more than she can comprehend. All she needed to do was to invite God into her life. Over the next few visits, we continued to talk and pray, and she invited Jesus into her life. The last time I saw her before she died, she had an angelic, peaceful quality about her, and although she could barely whisper, she assured me that she was praying and would be just fine.

"After her death, her family thanked me for helping Stella find the Lord. Interestingly, they indicated that they tried to do the same thing but had been told that her friend, Ruth, was already providing for Stella's spiritual needs. I had finally said yes to be used as an instrument of God's love and caring."

A Link in the Chain

Clem Richardson of Salinas, California, had a business associate, John, who was dying of ALS (Lou Gehrig's disease). Clem was a member of Christians in Commerce, and he invited John to some CIC events, but he declined. It was reported that he also declined any effort to seek reconciliation with God.

"My wife and I continued to pray for John," Clem says. "I also visited him over his last few months. At his request, his friends organized a fund-raiser auction and barbecue at his ranch to benefit ALS. At the auction one of his friends brought a priest along as a guest. The priest and John formed a quick friendship, and John ended up receiving the sacraments of reconciliation and anointing of the sick before he died.

"At John's funeral I was convinced that God had won the war for John's soul. Even though I was unsuccessful in recruiting John to Christian gatherings, God used my effort as a link in the chain to bring John back to him."

Clem concludes, "We must always keep trying no matter how things look or how weak our efforts appear. God will always use them for his greater purpose."

In his association with CIC, Clem has a long history of inviting numerous people over the years to Challenge Weekends. After attending his first Challenge Weekend, he prepared a list of twenty-eight friends and relatives whom he thought would benefit; eventually he invited all of them, and several attended. As time passed he invited others, including work associates, classmates from college, and more friends and family. "As I looked at the names," Clem said, "I realized how many opportunities I have missed through the years. Although there were many who came, there were also many unsent or weak invitations. I had given up on some and judged that others would not respond. I was convicted that my own pride made the list my own, rather than the one God provided me. Still, there is much joy in helping those I love move to a closer relationship with Jesus and sharing a wonderful weekend experience. Among the family members that attended was my father (now deceased), who said at the time he was too old to change. I praise Jesus for every name on my list, and though I have a long way to go, I plan to urgently reach out to the other lives Jesus wants to change."

Jesus says, "I am the way, the truth and the life" (Jn 14:6). He has the answer to the problems we find in the world and in our workplaces. He has the solution to anger, discord, jealousy, selfish ambition, greed, alcohol and drug addictions, sexual immorality, marital infidelity, lying, deceit, depression, and sloth. People experiencing these afflictions need Jesus. Many are in our workplaces.

On the day of Pentecost after the disciples had received the baptism in the Holy Spirit, Peter pleaded with the more than 3,000 who had gathered, "Save yourselves from this corrupt generation" (Acts 3:40). Our generation is not much different from the generation of the first century in terms of the above afflictions and living outside of the will of God. The people asked Peter, "What shall we do?" His answer is just as applicable today as it was then. "Repent and be baptized in the name of Jesus Christ for the forgiveness of your sins. And you will receive the gift of the Holy Spirit" (Acts 3:38). The promise of the Holy Spirit and its transforming impact on our lives still holds true for us today and for all whom we lead to the Lord by word and example.

Out of love for God and compassion for the people he places in your life, you can seize the opportunities to reach out, just as Ken, Ruth, and Clem did. The stakes are high and the consequences eternal.

Questions for Reflection or Discussion

1. How has your conduct impacted your work environment?

2. In the course of carrying out your work responsibilities, do you consider how you can serve others in your workplace?

3. Would people in your workplace know you are a Christian by your conduct?

4. Has anyone ever asked you for the reason for your joy or peace? How have you responded?

5. Has anyone ever shared a problem with you or sought your advice on non-business matters? How were you able to help them?

6. Have you ever joined with others in your workplace to pray for colleagues or your employer? If not, could you see this happening?

7. If you have been wronged by a boss or colleague, have you been able to forgive him or her? If you have wronged or offended a colleague, have you been able to apologize and seek forgiveness? Describe.

8. Would you be prepared to share your Christian faith with someone in your workplace if the opportunity arose? What would you say?

Chapter Six

THE KINGDOM IS NOW

There is a common notion among many Christians that the kingdom of God is only something to be experienced after death. Yes, if we abide in God and seek to do his will, there is a heaven that awaits us upon our passing from this life, a resurrection that follows, and an eternal life with the Father in a new creation. But so much of what Jesus said to his disciples and the people of his day exhorted them to do something with this life in order to advance the creation that God had inaugurated and Jesus had redeemed. As a part of the prayer Jesus taught the disciples to pray, he instructed them to ask the Father that "your kingdom come, your will be done on earth as it is in heaven" (Mt 6:10). Jesus gave us a model prayer that had as its first petition a request for the kingdom of God to come on this earth here and now, as it is in heaven.

When the Pharisees asked Jesus when the kingdom of God would come, Jesus said, "The kingdom of God does not come with your careful observation, nor will people say, 'Here it is,' or 'There it is,' because the Kingdom of God is within you" (Lk 17:20-21). Jesus told the Pharisees that the kingdom of God had already come through him. When we accept Jesus as the Son of

God and are "born again...of water and spirit" (Jn 3:3, 5), we enter the kingdom of God.

Understanding the Kingdom through the Parables

Most of the parables that Jesus told in the Gospels describe what the "kingdom" is like and how it is manifested in this life.

- The kingdom of God requires its people to be open to receiving God's Word (The Parable of the Sower, Mt 13:1-23).

- The kingdom is not static but is always growing (The Parables of the Growing Seed and Mustard Seed, Mk 4:26-34).

- The kingdom intersects with evil and grows along side it (The Parable of the Weeds, Mt 13:24-30).

- The kingdom must mix with the world in order to be a leavening agent (The Parable of the Yeast, Mt 13:33).

- The kingdom is about reaching out to those who do not know God (The Parables of the Lost Sheep and Coin, Lk 15:1-10).

- The kingdom involves our accepting God's invitation (The Parable of the Wedding Banquet, Mt 22:1-14).

- The kingdom requires forgiving one another (The Parable of the Unmerciful Servant, Mt 18:21-35).

- The kingdom expects us to use—not bury—the love and talents God gives us to further his creation and grow his kingdom (The Parable of the Talents, Mt 25:14-30).

In The Parable of the Mustard Seed, Jesus asks, "What shall we say the kingdom of God is like? It is like a mustard seed, which is the smallest seed you plant in the ground. Yet when planted, it grows and becomes the largest of all garden plants, with such big branches that the birds of the air can perch in its shade." Jesus isn't describing some future event but a present-day reality. Both individually and collectively, he is describing how we experience the kingdom. It usually starts small. Then, it must grow if we are to experience its fruit in our life and become the means to welcome and guide others to its branches.

In the Parable of the Yeast, Jesus said, "The kingdom of heaven[1] is like yeast that a woman took and mixed into a large amount of dough." We are the yeast and the dough is the world. As yeast, we must mix with the world, including the workplace, if we are to be the leavening agents God calls us to be. As the yeast transforms the dough, so we are to transform our workplaces.

In the Parable of the Weeds, Jesus says the kingdom "is like a man who sowed good seed in his field. But while everyone was sleeping, his enemy came and sowed weeds among the wheat, and went away. When the wheat sprouted and formed heads, then the weeds also appeared." When the servants asked if he wanted them to pull up the weeds, he said no, "because while you are pulling the weeds, you may root up the wheat with them. Let both grow together until the harvest. At that time I will tell the harvesters: First collect the weeds and tie them in bundles to be burned; then gather the wheat and bring it into my barn." During the current age, the sons of God and the sons of the evil one will be seen working side by side in this world. We should not be surprised if we are surrounded by people with a dominant concern for self who are morally confused, chasing after empty measures of success, and acting as if God does not exist. But through Jesus Christ who is in us and by the power of the Holy Spirit, we have the opportunity to redeem the people and circumstances surrounding us. Then at the harvest (resurrection), we will be gathered into the barn of the new heaven and new earth that Jesus promises.

In Matthew 6:25-33, Jesus exhorts us not to worry about food or clothing, the things of this life. Rather, he says we should first seek the kingdom of God and his righteousness and all these things will be given to us as well. Seeking and building the kingdom of God should be our first priority—now, in this life—and he will give us what we need to live.

God Working in History through His People

God has always been involved in the major movements of history. He called Abraham to raise a people to whom he would reveal himself. He called Moses and the prophets of the Old Testament to provide guidance on how this people should live. He sent his son, Jesus, born of a woman, who became one of us to obtain victory over Satan and death, and be a means to provide forgiveness and freedom from our sins. By God's great act of love in the death and resurrection of his Son and the outpouring of the Holy Spirit, he has empowered us to continue to build his kingdom. As N.T. Wright suggests, God was "restoring creation under the wise rule of a renewed human being."[2]

Jesus' birth, life, death, and resurrection took place at a given time and place in history. We have far more evidence of this in the writings of his contemporaries and the witnesses of his day than the evidence required by our system of criminal justice to convict a person of first degree murder. Paul reports that after appearing to Peter and then to the apostles, Jesus "appeared to more than five hundred of the brothers at the same time, most of whom are still living" (1 Cor 15:6). Wright says people witnessing Jesus in his resurrected body contributed more than any other factor to spurring the growth of the early Church.[3]

Since the time of Jesus, we have continued to see God at work throughout history. We see him at work in the timing of Jesus' coming, when the Roman Empire was at its zenith with its vast system of roads and commerce to facilitate the growth of the early Church. The conversion of the Roman Emperor Constantine provided official recognition for the Church. The monastic movement preserved Christianity and learning during the Dark Ages; its monasteries evangelized the barbarians and became the cultural centers for life, learning, and commerce, all of which provided the foundation of Western civilization. The pilgrims, the Jesuits, the Franciscans, and other religious groups brought Christianity to the new world. In the last century, God worked through his people in the defeat of Nazi Germany and the collapse of the Soviet Union. Recent decades have seen the rise of the civil rights movement for black Americans.

While these examples are rather sweeping and general in scope and may not reflect the Father in every detail, the point is that God works through those who respond to his call to bring his presence to bear on the circumstances and events of this life and the history of this world. David J. Bosch says in his book, *Transforming Mission*, "Salvation history is not a separate history, a separate thread itself inside secular history. There are not two histories, but there are two ways of understanding history. The Christian is not preoccupied with a different set of historical facts, but uses a different perspective. The secular historian will turn historical facts into profane history, whilst the believer will see the hand of God also in secular history."[4]

The Significance of a Globalized Commerce

The dominance of business and commerce in today's world, with its far reaching global influence, is one of these major movements in history. From the dawn of civilization and for several millennia, business consisted primarily of an agrarian culture with individual farmers and craftsmen offering goods and services to the local village. As shipping and transport grew, trade began to take place between nations. The Industrial Revolution, which brought about the means to manufacture a multitude of products on a large scale, provided further impetus for trade among nations.

The explosion of information technology in the last two decades has made business and commerce one of the dominant social institutions of our times. Its globalized nature transcends all national, language, ethnic, and cultural boundaries. My former company, ExxonMobil, operates in 132 countries in every region of the world. But today, it is not just large companies that have international operations. The Internet enables even an individual entrepreneur to reach out to the global marketplace. The pervasive nature of business and commerce touches everyone who works or purchases a product or service. God is involved in all of this through his people, moving his creation forward, reaching lives, and impacting areas that may never intersect directly with the institutional church.

Kingdom Builders

Brian Couch, after holding several engineering positions for Honeywell in South Bend, Indiana, was given the opportunity to become general manager of a Honeywell plant manufacturing aerospace parts in Kingman, Arizona. With their four children, Brian and his wife, Beth, left behind a close-knit bunch of relatives, good schools, and other Christian friends who were like family. For the Couches, the environment in Kingman was very different. Brian reports that family strife and domestic violence were not uncommon. The dropout rate at one of the local high schools was 35 percent over four years. There was very little sense of community.

All of this was also reflected in the factory Brian was asked to manage. Quarrels between workers were common. Backbiting, gossip, rough language, and conflict were prevalent. There were no means for settling disputes. There was no sense of teamwork. There was little trust between management and workers, or among the workers themselves. Husbands and wives were even reported to have called supervisors to gather divorce fodder on their spouses.

After Brian arrived and observed all of these conditions, he called together his newly assembled leadership team and told them that certain kinds of speech—vulgarity, gossip, ruining a person's reputation—would no longer be tolerated. He said the same thing in a subsequent all-factory meeting with employees. He initiated procedures to settle disputes between employees and disagreements between employees and management. He instituted incentives and bonuses for workers who met performance and safety objectives. He encouraged employees to enroll in college correspondence courses. He gave his employees a vision of how their factory was connected to the outside world—how the airplane parts they were manufacturing could end up in planes carrying their own relatives.

He began hosting quarterly all-factory social events in order to boost morale, build relationships, and let the workers know he was invested in them. Usually the whole Couch family would show up at these events, and he encouraged the employees to bring their families. At one such gathering, following a year of increased profitability for the plant, Brian's leadership team bought twelve-ounce rib-eye steaks and then stood behind the grills, cooking the steaks to order as each employee came by.

The Couches also had an impact on Kingman outside the factory with neighbors, other families, and young people who came in contact with the Couch children. Beth organized prayer sessions with neighbors and other mothers. Brian and Beth have set an example for supporting their children by hosting parties where the kids can have fun but not get into trouble.

If you are thinking that the Couches' move to Kingman was just another corporate transfer, you would be missing the deeper meaning of what was going on. Things changed in this factory, and the difference could be directly linked to Brian's arrival. There was something behind what Brian was doing and how he was acting. He was allowing the presence of Christ in him to be manifested to his employees by treating them with respect, setting up mechanisms for reconciling disputes, encouraging personal development and training, rewarding good work, and bringing truth and fairness into the dealings between management and workers. The factory's performance improved, with a 33 percent increase in sales and a 75 percent increase in profitability. Though Brian never outwardly proclaimed the name of Jesus in his official capacity as general manager, Christ was working through him, bringing his love, healing, and truth to the employees of this factory and in his careful overseeing of the efficient production of aerospace parts used by the larger society.

The Kingdom Is Now

Brian and his family were building God's kingdom in Kingman, Arizona. That's the way God works—through people like Brian and Beth. You don't have to be a general manager of a factory to have this kind of impact, either; anyone at any level can be Christ to the people and circumstances in their workplaces.

Questions for Reflection or Discussion

1. How do you perceive the kingdom of God? Is it something you can experience only after you die and go to heaven, or is it something you can experience today?

2. What are some examples of experiencing the kingdom of God in your life? In your workplace?

3. As in the Parable of the Sower, does your life provide good soil in which the Word of God can grow? Think of times when this has happened.

4. As in the Parable of the Yeast, think of examples of how your life has been a leavening agent for God's kingdom in the world and your workplace.

5. Can you think of other examples of God working through his people to affect the major movements of history?

6. Do you believe commerce, with the explosion of information technology, globalization, and its reach into everyone's life, is a major movement of history that God wishes to impact?

7. What steps can you take to make the kingdom of God more of a present-day reality in your workplace?

Chapter Seven

YOU CAN BRING HOPE TO YOUR WORKPLACE

Every Christian has the opportunity to be Christ and bring transformation and hope to his or her workplace. We can build the kingdom of God right where we are. Business owner and employee, blue collar and white collar, management and front-line worker, educator and professional—each of us can transform where we work—offices, factories, farms, warehouses, retail stores, transportation services, armed forces, schools, hospitals—into places where the love and power of Christ is present and goods and services are produced with excellence.

You may think that this is not possible in your workplace, or that it would not be allowed. You may think that you are not capable of having such an impact. The many stories in this book demonstrate that everyday Christians just like you are indeed making an impact and bringing transformation and hope to their workplaces. If you look behind each of these stories you will find certain characteristics common to the people involved.

- They have a personal relationship and friendship with God.

- They have experienced the power of the Holy Spirit in their lives.

- They seek God's will in how they conduct their lives.

- They allow God to work through them to bring his love and truth to the people and circumstances in their lives.

Let's look at each of these characteristics and how they can become a part of your life, so that you, too, can bring transformation and hope to your workplace.

Friendship with God

In order for us to allow God to work through us, we need to have a relationship with him. In order for us to be his agent in the workplace, we need to *know* him, not just *know about* him. Through our baptism and saying "yes" to Jesus and believing in his name, we have received Jesus Christ and the Holy Spirit, but we may still not have an ongoing, day-to-day relationship with him. We may regularly attend church and still not have an active relationship with God, the Father. We may be the beneficiary of his grace, but still not experience the fullness of his presence. As I've shared, it wasn't until I was thirty-seven years old, after having been a Christian all my life, that I began to have an ongoing relationship with God through Jesus Christ.

God's offer of friendship is open to anyone. Your response usually begins with a desire on your part to come to know him, seeking forgiveness for sin and committing or recommitting your life to him. Additionally, you can ask Jesus to fill you with the power of the Holy Spirit, who opens up to you the mind and heart of God. Finally, you can spend time with him through prayer and conversation. Jesus says, "You are my friends if you do what I command. I no longer call you servants, because a servant does not know his master's business. Instead, I have called you friends because every-

thing that I learned from my Father I have made known to you"
(Jn 15:14-15).

How amazing! The God of all creation offers each of us
friendship and a position in his business: building his kingdom
on earth in our time and place. To begin this relationship requires
no special training—just a decision, a decision to accept his offer
in faith, seek forgiveness for your sins, and acknowledge your need
and dependence on Jesus Christ. A good friend once said to me, "I
am in awe of how present God has truly been in my life, but then
I didn't really notice his presence until I became present to him."

If you have not experienced God's presence in your life, or if
that presence has been an on-again, off-again type of relationship, or if you have compartmentalized your life by putting God
in a box that you open only on Sunday, simply pray, "Lord Jesus, I
want to be your friend. I want to be present to you and have you
be present to me. Forgive me for my sins and take them from me.
I surrender my life to you and pray that you will build my faith to
enable my will to become your will."

Like any relationship, you need to spend time with God for
your relationship with him to grow. The Gospel of John says,
"Now this is eternal life: that they may know you, the only true
God and Jesus Christ whom you have sent" (Jn 17:3). Prayer is
essential; make an appointment, just like you do for all important
meetings. When I was working for Mobil, my appointment was
6:30 to 7:00 a.m. during the week. Now that I have a more flex-
ible schedule, it is usually between 7:00 and 8:00 a.m. If you have
never set time aside each day to pray, start out with a commitment of at least ten minutes and let the time expand as you and
the Lord grow closer. The Father and the Son want to engage
you in conversation. They want to speak to you, and they want

you to speak freely and openly to them. As you share your life with them, you'll come to know God as well as yourself. God created you to be drawn to him because you are incomplete without him. When asked what the greatest commandment was, Jesus said, "Love the Lord your God with all your heart and with all your soul and with all your mind" (Mt 22:37). The psalmist said, "For you created my inmost being; you knit me together in my mother's womb. I praise you because I am fearfully and wonderfully made; your works are wonderful, I know that full well" (Ps 139:13-14).

While the manner and content of your daily prayer will vary, it can include the following elements:

- Express your love, honor, praise and thanks to God (see Mt 6:9).

- Offer up your day and all that you may be doing.

- Repent of any sin (see Mt 6:12).

- Listen to God and reflect on his Word in Scripture, in your circumstances, spoken to you through others, and in the stillness of your heart. When reading the Gospels, ask Jesus to reveal himself to you.

- Seek his will in all that you do.

- Bring him your needs and concerns (see Philippians 4:6).

- Have confidence that your prayers are heard (see Mt 7:7-11).

Experiencing the Power of the Holy Spirit

It is through the Holy Spirit that the presence of the Father and the Son become real to us. It is through the Holy Spirit that we gain wisdom, knowledge, understanding, and counsel as God speaks to our heart and mind to guide our actions. It is through the Holy Spirit that we are empowered to act with love, fortitude, and faith. The Holy Spirit is Jesus' legacy to us. The Book of Acts tells how Jesus told the disciples to wait in Jerusalem until the Holy Spirit came to them. He knew that they would not be able to build his church and "make disciples of all nations" without the power of the Holy Spirit. The Holy Spirit transformed them from men who ran for their lives at Jesus' arrest to men who courageously articulated and defended the faith, and who eventually laid down their lives on its behalf. It is the power of the Holy Spirit that enabled them to recall and record the words of Jesus in the Gospels, continue his teaching, heal and do miracles as Jesus did, and enable a fledgling Church to grow and survive against all odds, outlasting the Roman Empire, apostasies, and other counter-movements down through the ages. Similarly, in our day, we need to experience the release of the power of the Holy Spirit in our lives if we are to carry on the work of building God's kingdom in our lives, families, and workplaces.

We experience the fullness and the power of the Holy Spirit by simply asking for it. Remember what Luke 11:11-13 says: "Which of you fathers, if your son asks for a fish, will give him a snake instead? Or if he asks for an egg, will give him scorpion? If you then, though you are evil, know how to give good gifts to your children, how much more will your Father in heaven give the Holy Spirit to those who ask him?" I experienced a fresh outpouring of the Holy Spirit and renewal in my life when some Christian friends laid their hands on me and prayed with me. But God is not confined in how he releases his Spirit in us. There is no special formula. It can happen through the prayers of others, the sacraments of baptism or confirmation, the laying on of hands, or in the silence and privacy of your room. The main ingredient is the desire in your heart to seek the fullness of God's presence in your life without conditions. A possible prayer could be, "Lord Jesus, I desire to live in you and for you to be alive in me. Sinner that I am, I know that this cannot happen without your grace and power. I reject sin and Satan. I accept you as Lord and Savior. Release in me the full power of your Holy Spirit. With all my heart I say, 'Come Holy Spirit; pour out your gifts in me.'"

Seeking God's Will

Your life is filled with choices—some big, some small. Where will you go to school? What kind of career should you pursue? What job should you take? Should you change jobs? Should you accept a promotion or a transfer? Should you get married? All of these are significant life decisions, but then there are the daily choices. How do you relate to a coworker who is difficult to deal with? Do you tell the boss what he wants to hear, or the truth? Do you take the time to listen to a colleague who is hurting? How much reimbursement do you seek for a recent business trip? Do you put in extra hours to get a job done right? How can you balance the demands of your work life with your family life and other responsibilities?

The proof of your ongoing "yes" to God is in the daily choices you make. Jesus said and did only what he heard and saw the Father doing. He said, "I do nothing on my own but speak just what the Father has taught me. The one who sent me is with me; he has not left me alone, for I always do what pleases him" (Jn 8:28-30). Jesus lived by the Father's will. You, too, should seek God's will in all that you do through prayer, Scripture, and the circumstances of your life. In seeking God's will, you should know your own inclinations (especially the sinful ones) well enough to know when you are hearing God or following your own desires. Who are you trying to please in your decisions— yourself, others, or God?

Our decisions are made on the battlefield between two kingdoms. Everything from God bears the marks of God. Those things from the world, the flesh, and the devil bear the marks of sin. St. Paul juxtaposes the contrast of these competing influences in his letter to Galatians. "The acts of the sinful nature are obvious: sexual immorality, impurity and debauchery; idolatry, and witchcraft; hatred, discord, jealousy, fits of rage, selfish ambition, dissensions, factions and envy; drunkenness, orgies and the like" (Gal 5:19-21). But Paul goes on to say, "The fruit of the Spirit is love, joy, peace, patience, kindness, goodness, faithfulness, gentleness and self-control" (Gal 5:22-23). You can judge your choices by their fruit and into which of the above categories they fall.

Doing God's will in the course of your daily decisions takes courage, obedience, and humility. One of the many challenges in living out your faith in the workplace is being able to resist going with the flow when dealing with a strong-willed manager. It often means bucking conventional wisdom or stepping back from what seems to be the popular thing to do. Jesus bucked the conventional wisdom of the religious leaders of his day and ended up bearing the cross for us. You, too, may encounter the cross in carrying out God's will in your workplace. You may want to avoid it, but Jesus said, "If anyone would come after me, he must deny himself and take up his cross and follow me. For whoever wants to save his life will lose it, but whoever loses his life for me will find it. What good will it be for a man if he gains the whole world, yet forfeits his soul? Or what can a man give in exchange for his soul?" (Mt 16:24-26). You may need to follow some of the examples in this book, such as Douglas who put his job on the line to preserve integrity in his company's accounting practices. You may need to make a change in your career for the sake of your family as Greg Aitkens did. You may need to take on greater humility in how you manage your company or staff like John Aden.

St. Paul said, "Do nothing out of selfish ambition or vain conceit, but in humility consider others better than yourselves. Each of you should look not only to your own interests, but also to the interests of others. Your attitude should be the same as Christ Jesus: Who being in the very nature of God, did not consider equality with God something to be grasped, but made himself nothing, taking the very nature of a servant" (Phil 2:3-7).

In an analysis of great companies, author Jim Collins found that humility was one of the characteristics common to the CEOs who led great companies.[1] Only eleven out of 1,435 companies studied were determined to be great as measured by cumulative returns at least three times the market over a period of fifteen years. Collins reports in his book, *Good to Great*, that those who worked with or wrote about the leaders in these eleven companies used words such as "quiet, humble, modest, reserved, shy, gracious, mild-mannered, self-effacing, understated, did not believe his own clippings," and so forth. In contrast to their counterparts in the good companies to which they were compared, Collins says, "The good-to-great leaders never wanted to become larger-than-life heroes. They never aspired to be put on a pedestal or become unreachable icons. They were seemingly ordinary people quietly producing extraordinary results."[2]

When we seek God's will in all things, we become willing to submit all areas of our life to him, giving him permission to guide our relationships, our time and work, our money and possessions, our future and reputation, and our liberty and will. By doing so, we are transformed from the inside out and able to transform the world around us. "Therefore, I urge you, brothers, in view of God's mercy, to offer your bodies as living sacrifices, holy and pleasing to God—this is your spiritual act of worship. Do not conform any longer to the pattern of this world, but be transformed by the renewing of your mind. Then you will be able to test and approve what God's will is – his good, pleasing and perfect will" (Rom 12:1-2).

"My Ministry Is the Marketplace"

Bill Colegrove is CEO of aspenhome™, a furniture company operating extensively in the United States and Asia, with its headquarters in Phoenix, Arizona. With revenues exceeding nine figures and approximately 6,000 people who work directly or beneficially for aspenhome™, Bill sees himself as a steward of what God has entrusted to him and his company.

"My ministry is the marketplace, my desk is his altar, and I have become his priest," says Bill. "While my goal personally is to lead a life pleasing to God, what we are individually becomes who we can be collectively. So my desire is that the organization for which I am responsible is pleasing to God as well. He leads me by his Holy Spirit, and the more I grow in unity with his Spirit, the more I see my work as Christ sees it. This manifests itself in the production of high quality furniture with excellent service through efficient distribution systems, but it also becomes visible in how we deal with our employees, suppliers, and customers."

An example is what took place during the 2008-2009 recession, which had a devastating effect upon the furniture industry. In the midst of widespread layoffs throughout the industry, no employee was laid off at aspenhome™ in either the US or China. Bill and his top leaders gathered their people together and sought their cooperation in foregoing raises and eliminating waste and redundancy. At the end of 2009, they held an emotional employee gathering with a spectacular celebration for working together to save each other's jobs and sustain the company.

God's Spirit is also present in how employees show concern for one another. "We had a manager in China who lost her husband due to a fatal heart attack," Bill reports. "Many of her fellow employees stepped forward to support her and her son. They raised money for her, which was then matched by the company. She was so overwhelmed by the love and support she received that she has since become a Christian.

"We've had other employees in China who have become Christians, not through any expressed efforts of proselytizing but simply through the example of some of our Christian employees and their conduct. A key senior official of our logistics company in China gave her life to the Lord a couple of years ago simply based on observing how some of our Christian employees were different from what she saw in an area where multiple cultures and religions intersect. This goes on throughout the company, involving people diverse in nationality, ethnic background, gender, and age. It occurs not by what people say but how they live— a little like the quote attributed to St. Francis, 'Preach the gospel always and only if necessary, use words.'

"Another area in which we seek to lead a corporate life pleasing to God is through our tithing and corporate citizenship work.

Yes, we do tithe from our earnings. This is something that I would have never thought about ten years ago. One of the beneficiaries of this effort is the City of Hope Comprehensive Cancer Care Center, located outside Los Angeles, providing medical care, spiritual support, and research for cancer patients. We donate directly and help them fund-raise responsibly through various efforts and programs, including Walks for Cancer. Last year we gave additional discounts to our retailers on their furniture purchases from aspenhome™, provided that they agreed to donate 50 percent of the discounts to City of Hope. We also encourage our employees to take on a spirit of service in support of various needs of their choice." As a result of these efforts aspenhome™ was recognized by the furniture industry with the Spirit of Life Award for Corporate Citizenship in 2009 and Supplier of the Year in 2008.

"We have a board and an executive team who are the gatekeepers of the culture we have developed," Bill says. "While seeking everyday professional excellence, they have a heart turned outward that serves both the bottom line and society. The marketplace has grown in importance to God. Two-wage-earner families are spending more of their time there. So it makes sense that God is equipping more leaders in the marketplace to build his kingdom and advance his creation."

Bill Colegrove is allowing God to work through him, bringing the presence of God and his truth, love, and excellence to his company. This is transforming his company and having an impact on employees, suppliers, customers, and the furniture industry. By providing a needed service to society in the manufacture and distribution of furniture, he is being a faithful steward, tending the garden and advancing creation just as God originally intended.

Just as God needed to become incarnate in Jesus to save the world, we must let Jesus become incarnate in us so that we can continue the work of bringing God's presence to a world in desperate need of his grace. The workplace is full of people whose lives may never intersect with the Church, but they intersect with you. Every day you have opportunities to be the Father's present-day incarnation by reflecting his love, integrity, and service to the people and circumstances you encounter in your lives. Out of love for God and for those who struggle without him, you can make yourself available to be used by God to expand his kingdom wherever he has placed you.

Billy Graham said, "I believe that one of the next great moves of God is going to be through believers in the workplace."[3] Blessed John Paul II, in his first sermon as pope, said, "Brothers and sisters, don't be afraid to welcome Christ and to accept his power. Help...all those who wish to serve Christ and, with the power of Christ, to serve man and the whole human race."[4]

Pray for the people and circumstances in your workplace. Ask God how he wants you to relate to a coworker, your boss, or employees that report to you. Ask him to help you do a better job, whatever your responsibilities. Ask him to give you the courage to uphold integrity in your business processes. Ask him to help you remain humble in your successes and not be defensive in your failures.

Be on the lookout for other Christians in your workplace so that you can support one another. When Jesus sent out the "seventy-two" in Luke 10:1-24, he sent them two by two. It is hard to build God's kingdom by yourself; God intended it to be done in the context of community. Look for Christian fellowship and support outside of your workplace, too—your church, a Christian community, or a workplace ministry. There are many ministries and groups being raised up by God today who focus on living out their Christian faith in the world.

Just as God the Father was in Jesus, so he wishes to reside in us. He wants you to be his presence in the world today. He wants you to bring that presence to your workplaces, families, and all of the circumstances of your lives. This has been his plan ever since his incarnation in Jesus and the outpouring of the Holy Spirit on the Day of Pentecost. By allowing him to dwell in you through the Holy Spirit, you give him permission to work through you. God will never force himself on you, but he is always ready to enter and be a part of your life and to enable you to bring his truth and love into the circumstances of your lives.

St. Paul said it so eloquently, "The mystery that has been kept hidden for ages and generations…is Christ in you, the hope of glory" (Col 1:26-27).

This is the hope for the workplace—Christ in you, living in you, working through you.

Questions for Reflection or Discussion

1. What characteristics are common to the people whose stories illustrate the theme of this book—bringing hope and transformation to the workplace?

2. How can you strengthen your relationship (friendship) with God?

3. How can you change your daily schedule to make an appointment with God, setting a time and place to talk with him each day?

4. Do you believe Jesus' words in John 14:12 that anyone who has

faith in him will do what he did and even greater things so he can bring glory to the Father?

5. Have you ever experienced the Holy Spirit enabling you to understand a truth, discern right and wrong motivations, have the courage to act or speak the truth, love someone who may not be lovable, give counsel or pray with a person in need, or speak about Jesus when the opportunity arose?

6. How do you seek God's will in your daily choices? Do you seek his guidance in prayer, in Scripture, in the circumstances of your life, in the words of others?

7. What are some examples when you have allowed God to work through you to impact decisions, lives, or the environment of your workplace?

8. Think of three things you can do to bring hope and transformation to your workplace.

ENDNOTES

Introduction

1. Os Hillman, *The 9 to 5 Window* (Ventura, CA: Regal Books, 2005), p. 23.
2. John Paul II, *Christifideles Laici* (Boston: Pauline Books & Media, 1988), p. 37.

Chapter 1

1. Jill Andresky Fraser, *White Collar Sweatshop* (New York: W. W. Norton & Company, Inc., 2001), pp. 3, 4, 5.
2. Cynthia Cooper, *Extraordinary Circumstances* (Hoboken, NJ: John Wiley & Sons, Inc., 2008), pp. 363, 364.
3. "See G. K. Chesterton, Orthodoxy, Popular classics Publishing, 2012, p. 8. "Certain new theologians dispute original sin, which is the only part of Christian theology that can really be proved."
4. Human Resource Institute, "A Global Study of Business Ethics," 2005, conducted for the American Management Association.
5. Michael Novak, *The Spirit of Democratic Capitalism* (Ontario: Madison Books, 1991), p. 56; hard cover edition published by Simon & Schuster, 1982.
6. Todd Sinelli, *True Riches* (Santa Cruz, CA: Lit Torch Publishing, 2001), pp. 18, 24, 25, 27.
7. Chuck Colson, *How Now Shall We Live* (Wheaton, IL: Tyndale House Publishers, Inc., 1999), p.135.
8. Second Vatican Ecumenical Council, Pastoral Constitution on the Church in the Modern World, *Gaudium et spes*, 43.
9. John Paul II, *Christifideles Laici* (Boston: Pauline Books & Media, 1988), 59.
10. Christians in Commerce (www.christiansincommerce.org) is an international ecumenical Christian ministry to the marketplace, with men's and women's chapters and small groups in the US and central Africa, first organized in 1983, with headquarters in Falls Church, Virginia.
11. Cynthia Cooper, *Extraordinary Circumstances*, (Hoboken, NJ: John Wiley & Sons, Inc., 2008), Introduction.
12. Anamika Gupta, "What Happened to Enron?" EzineSeeker.com, May 9, 2009.

13. Chad Bray, "Madoff Pleads Guilty to Massive Fraud," *The Wall Street Journal*, March 12, 2009.

Chapter 2

1. William A. Barry, SJ, *A Friendship Like No Other* (Chicago: Loyola Press, 2008), pp. 107, 193.
2. Cyril of Jerusalem, quoted in the *Catechism of the Catholic Church (CCC)*, 2782.
3. St. Augustine, In Ioann. Evang. Tract., 21, 8: CCL 36,216; see also *Christifideles Laici* (Boston: Pauline Books & Media, 1988), p. 43.
4. Martin Luther, *Union with Christ: The New Finnish Interpretation of Luther*, ed. by Carl E. Braaten and Robert W. Jenson (Grand Rapids, Mich.: Wm. B. Eerdmans Publishing, 1998), quoterd in an article entitled "Why Is Luther So Fascinating? Modern Finnish Luther Research" by Tuomo Mannermaa, p. 15; Luther's works 26:129-30.
5. *Catechism of the Catholic Church*, 2nd ed., Copyright 1997 by United States Catholic Conference—Libreria Editrice Vaticana, 460.
6. N.T. Wright, *The New Testament and the People of God* (Minneapolis: Fortress Press, 1992), p. 97, 98.
7. Kevin and Dorothy Ranaghan, *Catholic Pentecostals* (Paramus, NJ: Paulist Press, 1969), p.142. See Chapter 6 for a full discussion on experiencing the "baptism in the Holy Spirit" as an extension or renewal of baptismal promises.
8. John Paul II, *Christifideles Laici* (Boston: Pauline Books & Media, 1988), 13.

Chapter 3

1. *CCC*, 2427.
2. Stefan Cardinal Wyszynski, *All You Who Labor* (Manchester, NH: Sophia Institute Press, 1995), p.35.
3. Lester DeKoster, *Work, the Meaning of Your Life*, 2nd edition (Grand Rapids: Christian's Library Press, 2010), p. 62.
4. Ibid., p. 2.
5. Ibid., pp. 2, 3.
6. Ibid., p. 41.
7. John Paul II, *Laborem Exercens*, http://www.vatican.va/holy_father/john_paul_ii/encyclicals/documents/hf_jp-ii_enc_14091981_laborem-exercens_en.html, Section 25, "Work as a Sharing in the Activity of the Creator."

8. Ibid.

9. Os Hillman, *The 9 to 5 Window* (Ventura, CA: Regal Books, 2005), p. 23.

10. Doug Sherman and William Hendricks, *Your Work Matters to God* (Colorado Springs: NavPress, 1987), p. 15.

Chapter 4

1. Brian Skoloff and Jane Warren; "BP Oil Spill Costs Grow," *Washington Post*, November 2, 2010.

2. Henry and Richard Blackaby, *Spiritual Leadership* (Nashville: Broadman & Holman Publishers, 2001), p. 125.

Chapter 5

1. Mark Green, *Thank God It's Monday* (Bletchley, England: Scripture Union, 2001), p. 14.

Chapter 6

1. While Mark and Luke use the term "kingdom of God," Matthew uses "kingdom of heaven" because it was the custom of Jewish people not to speak of God or refer to him directly. Matthew, a Jew, writing for a Jewish community used the word "heaven" as a substitute for God. N.T. Wright, *Jesus and the Victory of God* (Minneapolis: Fortress Press, 1996), pp.202-203.

2. Ibid., p. 216.

3. N.T. Wright, *Simply Christian* (New York: HarperCollins Publishers, 2006), p.113.

4. David J. Bosch, *Transforming Mission* (Maryknoll, NY; Orbis Books, 1991), p. 508.

Chapter 7

1. Jim Collins, *Good to Great* (New York: HarperCollins Publishers, Inc., 2001), p. 27, 30.

2. Ibid., p. 28.

3. Os Hillman, "The At Work Movement: Opening the 9 to 5 Window," www.faithintheworkplace.com.

4. Carl Bernstein and Marco Politi, *John Paul II, His Holiness* (New York: Doubleday, 1996), p. 181.

ABOUT THE AUTHOR

BILL DALGETTY spent most of his career as a senior and managing attorney for Mobil Corporation, where he served for over thirty-eight years. He is a past president and chairman of the board of Christians in Commerce International. Bill is married, with five children and twelve grandchildren.